"Cummins offers new visions of education and proven paths to realize those visions."

—Jonathan Kozol

Other books by Paul F. Cummins

- *Richard Wilbur*
- *Dachau Song:*
  The Twentieth-Century Odyssey of Herbert Zipper

For Mortal Stakes

Paul F. Cummins
& Anna K. Cummins

For Mortal Stakes

Solutions for Schools and Society

PETER LANG
New York • Washington, D.C./Baltimore • Boston
Bern • Frankfurt am Main • Berlin • Vienna • Paris

Library of Congress Cataloging-in-Publication Data

Cummins, Paul F.
For mortal stakes: solutions for schools and society/
Paul F. Cummins & Anna K. Cummins.
p. cm. — (Counterpoints; v. 61)
Includes bibliographical references and index.
1. Education—Social aspects—United States. 2. Educational change—United
States. 3. Postmodernism and education—United States. I. Title. II. Series:
Counterpoints (New York, N.Y.); vol. 61.
LC191.4.C86   370'.973—dc21   97-19044
ISBN 0-8204-3811-1
ISSN 1058-1634

Die Deutsche Bibliothek-CIP-Einheitsaufnahme

Cummins, Paul F.:
For mortal stakes: solutions for schools and society/
Paul F. Cummins & Anna K. Cummins. –New York; Washington,
D.C./Baltimore; Boston; Bern; Frankfurt am Main; Berlin; Vienna; Paris: Lang.
(Counterpoints; Vol. 61)
ISBN 0-8204-3811-1

Published simultaneously by Bramble Company
4001 S. Decatur Blvd., #37-406, Las Vegas, NV 89103

Cover photo by Zelda Zinn.
Cover design by James F. Brisson.

The paper in this book meets the guidelines for permanence and durability
of the Committee on Production Guidelines for Book Longevity
of the Council of Library Resources.

© 1998 Peter Lang Publishing, Inc., New York

Printed in the United States of America.

Only where love and need are one,
And the work is play for mortal stakes,
Is the deed ever really done
For Heaven and the future's sakes.

–Robert Frost

Dedication

. . . To the vast and growing number of poor and voiceless children in America;

. . . To the students—past, present, and future—of Crossroads School and New Roads Schools;

. . . To Jack and Peter, my teachers; to Herbert, (April 27, 1904– April 21, 1997) my inspiration;

. . . To Emily, Anna, Julie, Paul & Conner, Liesl, Mimi & Ken, John, Jason & Debbie, Julie & Brian, Garrett, Jordan, and Audrey;

. . . To the memory of my father, Paul Stedman Cummins;

. . . To Ruthie & Lee;

. . . *To Mary Ann.*

Acknowledgements

First of all, I would like to thank my assistant, Adrienne McCandless, for typing and retyping version after version and for making many helpful suggestions.

Next, I want to thank Laurie Blum for believing in this book and for helping me navigate my way into the labyrinthine world of editing, promotion, and publication. I am also very grateful to Mr. Robert Withers for his wise and helpful suggestions in the early rounds of editing.

Once again, I want to thank Christopher Myers of Peter Lang Publishing for his confidence and cooperation, and his two wonderful project editors, Joe L. Kincheloe and Shirley R. Steinberg, for their excellent suggestions and wisdom. Also, I am indebted to Scott Gillam for his superb and detailed final copy editing. In addition, I want to thank Larry Bramble for his confidence and help.

There are many others to thank: Emily Cummins for providing an ongoing dialogue in the midst of her studies at Northwestern; Anna Cummins for her chapter on gender issues and for making this the basis of independent studies at Stanford; Anna, in turn would like to thank Estelle Freedman for her guidance, support, and wisdom in the Stanford Women's Studies Program; Tom Hickey for his help with my most difficult chapters—on funding school reform; Michele Hickey for her insights and suggestions; Linda de Kamberg Martinez for her help with the bibliography; Dawn Fairchild, Melissa Sweeney, Zelda Zinn, and Susan Cloke for assisting with the cover design; T. David Brent, editor, for his excellent questions and suggestions; Nat Reynolds for a twenty-five-year dialogue on education and life; Herbert Zipper for countless hours of discussing the book, chapter by chapter; Peter Levitt, whose insights help to broaden and deepen my arguments; Alva Libuser for her ideas and suggestions; Jack Zimmerman for his friendship and his teachings; Doug Thompson for editing many chapters; and finally, my old college roomie, John Carswell, for a wonderfully generous and helpful close reading and editing of the book.

Also, I want to acknowledge several of my own educational heroes who have inspired me over the years—Jonathan Kozol, Thomas Berry, Wendell Berry, Richard Wilbur, Daniel Smith (Stanford, Western Civilization 1955-56), Howard Gardner, Otis Pease, Alan Casson, Peter Levitt, Jack Zimmerman, and Herbert Zipper.

And finally, as always, to Mary Ann for her consistent example of integrity and passion in education and life and for her encouragement and love.

Grateful acknowledgment is made for permission to reprint "A Marshal Plan for Black America," which appeared in *KINESIS: A JOURNAL OF FICTION, POETRY, ESSAYS AND REVIEWS*, Volume 6, Issue 5, May 1997; and "A New Cosmology: Honoring the Blue Planet," which appeared in *THE TRUMPETER; JOURNAL OF ECOSOPHY*, Volume 13, No. 4, wn 53, 1996.

Also, thanks to Andrews and McMeel, a universal press syndicate company, for permission to reprint a chart on taxation found in *AMERICA, WHAT WHEN WRONG?* by Donald L. Barlett and James B. Steele.

Contents

Preface

Get busy living, or get busy dying.
                              —from *The Shawshank Redemption*

Above me a white butterfly is fluttering through the air
on wings that are its alone,
and a shadow skims through my hands
that is none other than itself, no one else's but its own.
When I see such things, I'm no longer sure
that what's important
is more important than what's not.
                              —Wisława Szymborska

He has half the deed done, who has made a beginning.
                              —Horace, *Epistles*, I.2.

The "Truth" is that American schools could become what all parents want for their children—enlightened, productive, and challenging. Of course, this is not what exists. We—citizens, parents, educators, *and* students—know that the reality is otherwise, ranging from the mediocre to the sordid. Why are things not better? Because we do not care? Because we do not know better or know what is wrong? Because our priorities are out of order? Because we lack leaders with vision and the courage to lead us where we all want to go if only someone would lead? Any of the above? I would say all of the above. And they are interrelated. We do not care because we do not know better and because our leaders are holding out wrong, unenlightened, or short-sighted solutions to major problems. Too often, schools are blamed for society's messes, and solutions are then sought at the school level rather than at the societal level where the mess was first created.

The problems of society and education are so intermeshed that it is impossible to talk of issues in the one arena without discussing the other. In California, for example, many public schools are underfunded and overcrowded. Yet these are conditions that are imposed upon the schools by changing immigration and demographic patterns, by elections in which the voters have lowered the property tax base for education and welfare, and in which school bonds have been voted down one after another. Drugs and gangs on campuses are related to multinational profiteering in the drug trade, and gangs flourish in part because of the disintegration of the family and the media's glorification of violence. Also, because of the underfunding and budget cutting, a host of engaging activities have been cut out of the curriculum, leaving in the wake a generation of angry and alienated young people. Where then do we point the finger?

The answer is certainly not just at the schools. The enemy is us: any citizen who has passively watched the deterioration of American schools and society, anyone who has actively voted from self-interest rather than for the common good. A host of educational reform movements are underway across the country; some good should come from this. But until we get a lot smarter about our nation's crisis and resolve to make sacrifices, act boldly, and confront the crisis directly and dramatically, we will achieve less than we can—or should. And so, our steady decline educationally, economically, culturally, and morally will continue.

Quite simply, we as a nation are neglecting/abusing our children. We may not be the first generation of adults to do so, but we have the poorest excuse in history. For us, it need not be so.

> Standing here by the Ohio River, watching it drift west into the edge of the horizon, picturing it as it flows onward to the place three hundred miles from here where it will pour into the Mississippi, one is struck by the sheer beauty of this country, of its goodness and unrealized goodness, of the limitless potential that it holds to render life rewarding and the spirit clean. Surely there is enough for everyone within this country. It is a tragedy that these good things are not more widely shared. All our children ought to be allowed a stake in the enormous richness of America. Whether they were born to poor white Appalachians or to wealthy Texans, to poor black people in the Bronx or to rich people in Manhasset or Winnetka, they are all quite wonderful and innocent when they are small. We soil them needlessly.
>
> Jonathan Kozol, *Savage Inequalities*, p. 233

The deplorable conditions in American schools could be radically and rapidly improved, if we had the will to do so. We have the wealth, the knowledge, the capacity to bring about immediate change. What are the problems? What could we do to meet them? What social, cultural, and moral commitments would we as a nation need to make to effect change?

This book offers a menu of ways in which we can re-vision our future. The chapters are not strictly sequential, nor in strict order of priority, although I believe they do offer a coherent vision and an interrelated set of arguments. Each chapter is a call for action in a given area: Some chapters focus solely on education, others deal with social and political changes needed if schools are to succeed and if our nation is to flourish. Some chapters will be quite brief—their purpose is to call attention to problems and potential solutions which others have discussed. Consequently, the bibliography to this book, while admittedly idiosyncratic, is, I believe, important.

My goal in this book is to speak to educators, politicians, and citizens at large. This is not meant to be yet another prophecy of doom nor is it professional monograph. It is a call to action and a setting forth of some simple and crucial means of restoring (in some cases) and revising (in others) programs and policies which serve children and young people best. In 1961, the United States decided to land a man on the moon. Eight years later, this remarkable feat was accomplished. Moreover, between 1969 and 1972, six American expeditions landed on the moon and twelve men walked its surface. If we can do this, surely we can resolve to overhaul and improve our schools.

FROM ALIENATION
TO ENGAGEMENT

Chapter 1

The Goals of Education:
What Is Truly Basic?

The purpose of life is life itself—
and when we have done our share inwardly,
the outer things will follow of themselves.
                    —Goethe, "Letter to Heinrich Meyer" (1792)

No longer good remembering names
the botanist greets
each flower
with a sigh.

                                        —Peter Levitt

In his poem "Audubon," Robert Penn Warren asks, "what is a man but his passion?" It is a good question for every person, every educator, and every school to address. Life is but a whisk between nonbeing and the time and space which lie beyond death. To spend the miracle of human consciousness, with its accompanying capacity for embracing life, in anything but a passionate commitment to life would be sad beyond words. The role of the educator and the school is to show students the way: to help each boy and girl, each young man and woman, to discover his or her unique capabilities, inclinations, curiosities, and to help ignite whatever spark is there into a full, blazing fire. The ultimate goal of education should be to help each student to say yes to life. Thus, schools must be places which offer wide-ranging and diverse classes, programs, and activities so that each student can experiment and come to his or her interests. The excitement that springs out of the discovery activity so often animates the young person in other spheres of life and learning. Thought patterns elaborate and ramify, such that the student who becomes *excited* about a line of poetry becomes alive to lines of good prose; the student who becomes curious about a science experiment becomes more curious about mathematical calculations; the student who becomes enthralled about the architecture of a musical composition becomes more interested in geometry and structure in all subjects.

When I first became headmaster of an elementary school in 1970, I made changes which caused instant parental apprehension: the children were coming home happy. How, therefore, could they be learning? I spent hours in individual conferences and public meetings reassuring parents that happiness was not an obstacle to learning; rather, it was essential.

Parents were, I believe, operating from a mindset they had "learned" in their own education: the purpose of elementary and secondary education is to prepare for *later* life—for college, for graduate school, for work, for a comfortable life style. It is a mindset born out of materialism and a sort of grim economic pragmatism. In this view, education is a means toward other ends, but not an end in itself.

Play as Education

Childhood, I would argue at these conferences, *is* an end in itself—a time of innocent celebration of life, of the universe. Play is not only the essence of childhood; it is the major form of exploration and learning of the child. To rob children of playful celebration not only deprives the child of his/her once-upon-a-time of "lamb white days," but it robs the adult which that child will ultimately become of feelings, of "intimations of immortality" to draw upon during the rest of life. Much as a pianist who does not study from ages four to eleven can never develop the flexibility of technique at a later age, so a child who has never had the oceanic sense of unity with all of life can never recapture those sensibilities which must come early in life. When the nurturing of passion and the quest for joy serve as the primary guidelines for schools, not only in designing curricula but in developing the school's ambiance, then the other traditional and intellectual considerations fall properly into place and are answered in ways more conducive to student growth.

Most students do not flunk out of life intellectually; they flunk out emotionally. They fail to discover any passion in life, and so failing, they find little joy in what they do. It is not enough to teach subjects or material to students; the conditions for discovery, the variety of activities, must be present in the schools. This leads to a related principle—the principle of engagement.

The students I worry about are the ones who are drifting from day to day, students who are not involved in the process of learning. The way to engage them is to make them active rather than passive learners. Ask a student to lead a class; to conduct peer tutoring sessions for younger students; to research and then implement a community service project—these are examples of ways to *engage* students. Alfred North Whitehead states that learning must be useful; the student must see some reason for learning what she is being asked to learn; "Education is the acquisition of the art of the utilization of knowledge" (1929: 16). By this, Whitehead did not mean a sort of 1960s notion of political relevance (for one thing, his book was written in 1929); rather, he meant that knowledge cannot be meaningful if it becomes inert. It must be kept alive through application: "the pupils have got to be made to feel they are studying something, and are not merely executing intellectual minuets" (21). Of course, as further evidence of the interconnectedness of things, when the teacher brings passion and joy to the process, the pupils feel they are studying 'something.'

Teachers do have one thing—in spite of our difficult school conditions—working in their favor: that is, the natural curiosity of children. Little children do not want to do rote activities; they want to explore, to play, to invent. The teachers who do turn their classrooms into a discovery land are a delight to behold. Rafe Esquith at Hobart Elementary School in midcity Los Angeles is one such teacher.

A Teacher for All Seasons

Hobart Elementary School (K–6) is the third largest elementary school in the Los Angeles Unified School District. It is a school of 2,300 children: 80 percent Hispanic, 17 percent Asian, 2 percent African American, and 1 percent other. Rafe Esquith teaches a class of forty students, fifth and sixth graders, most of whom are immigrant children who go home each evening to non–English-speaking families. His classroom, by his choice, lies at the back corner of the campus adjacent to a burnt out, graffiti-covered apartment building, the former home of gangs and major drug deals. He instructs his students to keep a low profile—not to carry around books or in any way reveal they are one of "Rafe's kids." Once, at a school assembly, he confessed that he had made the mistake of announcing a student's success in a citywide math competition. Within the hour, the student had been badly beaten up.

Rafe Esquith meets his students at 6:30 every morning; they stay until 5:00 in the evening. Over the blackboard in his room are two decorations: one is the quote "there are no shortcuts"; the other is a series of college pennants with a list below each one of his former students who attend those colleges—Stanford, University of Chicago, Berkeley, Notre Dame, Harvard, Swarthmore, et al. At lunchtime, they do not leave the room; instead they stay in class and Rafe teaches them guitar or computer skills. They read more than ten novels a year, i.e., Dickens, *A Christmas Carol*; Golding, *Lord of the Flies*; *The Diary of Ann Frank*; Richard Wright, *Black Boy*; Steinbeck, *Of Mice and Men*. He provides each of his forty students with their own paperback copy of each book—over 400 books, all paid for from out of his own pocket. He reinvests his salary in the class; he and his wife, a nurse, live on her salary. In addition to the novels, they do Shakespeare. Each year they read a complete play; they go over it line by line; they memorize passages; in the classroom converted to minitheatre they perform the entire play (this year, 1997—*A Winter's Tale*), and they perform it superbly. Actor Hal Holbrook attended a recent performance and was amazed. As if this were not enough, Esquith takes the entire class to the Old Globe in San Diego, to the Utah Shakespeare Festival (where they also go river-rafting), and during the summer, to Ashland, Oregon, for the Shakespeare Summer Festival. Again, he pays all the expenses—hotel, travel, meals, play tickets (they see five plays in Ashland).

The results are extraordinary. His students—remember these are fifth and sixth grade minority and mostly immigrant students—read beyond their years; they score at the top of citywide math tests; they read Shakespeare with understanding and delight. Two years ago, I watched his class perform *The Tempest*. Ariel was played by a Korean girl who had learned English only two years before. Caliban was a Hispanic boy who acted with humor and articulation. Prospero was a powerful Hispanic girl with a sophistication I marveled at. Passion, joy, engagement: the aims of education.

When these ingredients are present, education can move to deeper and deeper levels. Once engaged, teachers can help students gain an awareness of the importance of style. Once involved in a subject, students can be led to an aesthetic sensibility: "the love of a subject in itself and for itself pervades the whole being. The administrator with a sense of style hates waste; the engineer with a sense for style economizes his material; the artisan with a sense for style prefers good work. Style is the ultimate morality of mind" (Whitehead, 1929: 24). The awareness of style grows with the ability to think for oneself. Again, passionately engaged and joyful students are better able to think clearly. They are not weighed down with inert routine, boredom, pressure to perform on tests, and the like. They are free to range over broad issues and to delve into the specifics of complex matters with some idea of the forest and not just the individual trees. It is all interconnected: *critical thinking, developing a sense of style, joy, engagement, passion.*

The Four Goals of Education

Engagement for what? Passion for what? I would argue that there are four essentials which the educational skills of a given student, a given school should address: responsibility for future generations, posterity and survival of the planet; reverence for life and celebration of life; commitment to social justice; and commitment to living in joyful community with others. They are, of course, closely interrelated, but I believe some important distinctions may be drawn.

Responsibility to Posterity
The notion of posterity used to be a goal, a value, an end of education. Herbert Zipper, a friend and fellow educator, said on numerous occasions, "I want to be a good ancestor." Par-

ents understand this and will often devote their entire lives to making things better for their children. Now as the twentieth century gives way to the twenty-first, the notion of posterity takes on added meaning, for the very possibility of *having* a guaranteed future is under assault. The nuclear threat, while somewhat mitigated, remains, but even more critical is the ecological threat. Thus, one cannot work to make a better economic life for one's children without being aware of the ecological sword of Damocles hanging over humankind's head. As I will argue (in chapters 5 and 6), overpopulation, environmental degradation, and human inequalities are three interrelated threats both to future generations and to the very possibility of a human future on this planet. The twenty-first century might well be marked by continuing and worsening population crises, an escalation of ecological disasters, and mounting social injustice. An education which does not address these issues is at best foolish, at worst, immensely dangerous.

Reverence for Life

Now, because so many students are born, grow up in, and are educated in big cities divorced from any relationship to the land, a reverence for life must be an attendant value or goal of education. Albert Schweitzer provided an important spiritual apology for the concept of "reverence for life":

> The great fault of all ethics hitherto has been that they believed themselves to have to deal only with the relations of man to man. In reality, however, the question is what is his attitude to the world and all life that comes within his reach. A man is ethical only when life, as such, is sacred to him, that of plants and animals as that of his fellow men, and when he devotes himself helpfully to all life that is in need of help. Only the universal ethic of the feeling of responsibility in an ever-widening sphere for all that lives—only that ethic can be founded in thought. The ethic of the relation of man to man is not something apart by itself: it is only a particular relation which results from the universal one. (Schweitzer, 1933: 126)

But now we must add to Schweitzer's spiritual thinking the realization that there is even a selfish reason for teaching a reverence for all life: that is, without revering all of life, we will ultimately destroy that which sustains our very physical existence. So we celebrate and revere life because it is inherently good to do so and because it is necessary to our very survival.

Commitment to Social Justice

The third goal of education, a commitment to social justice, is also called for on both moral and pragmatic grounds. The United States Declaration of Independence and Constitution and the Judeo-Christian precepts upon which the nation was founded all proclaim the value and inherent worth of each and every individual. Allowing one-fourth of our children to grow up in poverty, tolerating the intolerable conditions of America's and the world's poor is, therefore, a direct contradiction to our own deepest values. Contradictions of this nature are ultimately ruinous to individuals as well as nations. We see the ruins already in the United States. Commentator after commentator, scholar after scholar, citizens' group after group—all are issuing jeremiads about the decay and disintegration of American and world society, and time and time again the lamentation is the same: too few are prospering; too many are suffering. However, the problem takes on even more dire proportions when we consider the sheer pragmatics of societal inequities. If the poor were to acquire and attain anything close to the wealth and material benefits of the few, the planet could not long endure the waste, pollution, destruction of rain forests, global warming, and other disasters which the few have already wreaked upon the earth. Somehow, greater equity in the possession and utilization of the earth's resources cries out for achievement. Social justice is thus not only a moral imperative, it is mandatory for the very survival of life on earth.

Again, we see the interconnectedness of all things—the arts are necessary for celebration, the humanities and history and social sciences are necessary to comprehend the human threats to society and the planet, and the sciences and math are needed to understand the physical and biological dimensions of our assault upon the earth.

Commitment to Community

Finally, I believe that once we make a greater commitment to social justice, we will begin to learn what the joys of living in a diverse community are. As long as the walls are high between rich and poor, white and nonwhite, caste and class, we will not hear the sounds of exotic music, of new poetry, of the stories of different peoples, and we will be limited to the sounds of only one song, one poem, one story. Walls breed suspicion, fear, and finally, boredom and sterility. Walls also lead to violence and wars.

We cannot survive and live in joyful community as a species unless our educational processes are widened and deepened. Finally, one must accept that there is a moral dimension to education which subsumes all else: that is, to learn the difference between right and wrong. C.S. Lewis in his study, *The Abolition of Man*, speaks of certain principles which are not simply value judgments, but which are value themselves. "Unless you accept these without questions," he writes, "as being to the world of action what axioms are to the world of theory, you can have no practical principles whatever. You cannot reach them as conclusions; they are premises." They are, he states, "not mere sentiments, but are rationality itself" (Lewis, 1947: 52, 44). Again, these principles, rationality itself, I would argue, are: (1) posterity, the responsibility for future generations, the survival of the planet; (2) the reverence and celebration of life; (3) a commitment to social justice; and (4) commitment to living in joyful community with others. These are the ends of education.

As a postscript, some will argue that the goal of education is happiness. And I would not disagree. I would argue, however, that unless the aforementioned principles inform one's education and one's life, true happiness is but an illusion.

Chapter 2

Anger and Alienation:
What to Do About It

When an individual is no longer a true participant, when he no longer feels a sense of responsibility to his society, the content of democracy is emptied. When culture is degraded and vulgarity enthroned, when the social system does not build security but induces peril, inexorably the individual is impelled to pull away from a soul-less society. This process produces alienation—perhaps the most pervasive and insidious development in contemporary society."

—Martin Luther King, Jr.

Gangs flourish when there's a lack of social recreation, decent education, or employment.

—Luis J. Rodriguez

Happiness. Responsibility for future generations. Social justice. Living in joyful community. These are not the hallmarks of American cities today. On the contrary, the signs of a breakdown in urban society are everywhere and are on the increase. Graffiti, race and gang wars, senseless acts of violence, eight- to twelve-year-olds committing murder, students bringing guns to class and shooting their teachers, senior citizens being mugged by preteen gangs—the newspapers and evening news are rife with such stories. Increasingly, similar stories directly touch the lives of everyone. One member of our private school board of trustees was robbed midday in her driveway in a "nice part of town"; another trustee had his windshield shot out by a freeway sniper. None of us are immune to such acts. Everyone bemoans "the youth of our day." Somehow, we perceive, they are different than we were. They seem so angry, so alienated from family, society, country. Their music is angry and their behavior is often antisocial, almost pathological. Why?

Explanations range from overindulgence to racism to the disintegration of culture and nation. Clearly there is truth here. In this chapter, I will focus, more narrowly, on the role that education plays in the problem—and, it is to be hoped, in the solution.

As I see it, we have removed (or in some ways failed ever to include) those parts of the school experience which *engage* young people. Students need to be actively involved in the learning process. Passivity leads to boredom. Passivity in overcrowded classes, conducted by overworked and demoralized teachers, in gang-infested, hostile-ugly-neighborhoods, leads to anger and alienation. Students should not have to sit in class after class doing little but listening to teachers talk or watching teachers struggle to keep control. Young people need to do things with their hands, to work in groups, to see the products of their labor, to create, to build, to produce something tangible, to have some sense that what they are doing is connected to life. I am not arguing for the 1960s' notion of "relevant," though that concept was often distorted and trivialized by its opponents. The key is not "relevant" so much as "alive". Stuffing 35–40 adolescents in a room for 50 minutes and expecting an overworked teacher to entertain them, even to teach them is, however, expecting the nearly impossible.

What to do? The initial—and obvious—move is to cut class sizes in half. This would enable teachers to take a host of actions they currently cannot do. These actions would include such basic things as: assigning and correcting essays on a regular basis, getting to know the individual needs of each student, assigning independent reading and science projects, individualizing math assignments, and on and on. A teacher who has 5 or 6 classes a day of 35–45 students in each class (with a total of 175–225) can do *none* of the above. A teacher who has 4 classes a day of 20 students each (80 total) can be a teacher. We can design as many reform programs as we like, we can expand technology in the classroom, but as long as we assign twice or thrice as many students to teachers as is reasonable, then we will not improve the quality of our schools. Students cannot speak out, cannot engage in productive discussion in overcrowded classrooms. So, they seek other avenues of self-expression-graffiti, crime, irresponsible and premature sexuality, drugs. Cut class size in half and you will see healthier forms of self-expression.

The second solution I offer to combat anger and alienation is related to the first. Put into the curriculum activities which *en*gage young people. At present, they are *dis*engaged. They are bored or frightened and feel that the education process has little meaning in their lives. They can see no connection between sitting in overcrowded classrooms and somehow ever improving their life situation. There are, however, four areas or programs which make these connections for the young and which actively engage them in their own education. We need to regard them not as extracurricular, but as essential to the well-being of our youth and our nation. They are:

1. The Arts (see chapter 3)
2. Community Service (see chapter 11)
3. Environmental Outdoor Studies (see chapter 7)
4. Human Development (see chapter 4)

The Arts

In his influential books, *Multiple Intelligences* and *Frames of Mind*, Howard Gardner (1993: 17-25) identifies seven kinds of intelligence. They are:

- verbal/linguistic
- logical/mathematical
- body/kinesthetic
- visual/spatial
- musical/rhythmic
- intrapersonal
- interpersonal

Schools tend to measure and accord importance only to the first two—verbal/linguistic and logical/mathematical. The other five are generally given short shift. Yet, three of these five involve the arts—dance (kinesthetic), visual arts (spatial) and music. By eliminating or reducing these areas from the curriculum, we discourage intelligent people from *expressing* their intelligence. We rob them of opportunities for gaining self-esteem and self-confidence. We deprive them of producing artifacts and giving recitals and discovering talents. The award-winning poet Jimmy Santiago Baca (1992), learned to write poetry in prison. There was no opportunity for this kind of expression in school. So, it turns out that even within linguistic intelligence we limit self-expression; creative writing is dismissed or just not done. How many Jimmy Bacas never learn that they have any talent at all in writing?

- Put the arts into the curriculum and we will reduce anger, the number of dropouts, and hence we will have fewer prisoners.
- Put the arts in the curriculum and we will reduce depression and alienation as students discover who they are and how to creatively and productively give voice or expression to their inner worlds.
- Put the arts in the curriculum and everyone in society benefits.

Community Service

Youth is a time of great idealism—or should be. Youth is a time when lasting values are formed. Youth is also a time of uncertainty and feelings of social irrelevance and uselessness. School to many young people is a meaningless exercise in futility. Young people want to feel needed, important, valuable. Community-service programs address all these problems. They also have another value: they often help *serve* the greater community.

Over the past twenty years as an educator, I have seen hundreds and hundreds of students transformed by their community-service activities. At my school, Crossroads School, community service is a graduation requirement, and scores of graduates have told me during and after college that it was their community-service project at Crossroads which gave focus to their college studies and, in many cases, gave them a clear sense of vocational direction. There is a story of a student who went to his zen master and said, "Master, I am depressed; what should I do?" The master replied, "encourage others." And, of course, this works with all of us—particularly with adolescents. When they are allowed to help others, they come alive in ways which are thrilling to behold. The best antidote to apathy and alienation is to find ways to *involve* students in experiences which transport them beyond their negative boundaries—intellectual, cultural, and geographic. Engaging them in activities designed to help others achieve multiple ends: it enhances each participant's sense of self-worth; it introduces the notion of community building and responsibility; it combats a hopelessness which many young people feel; it involves students in learning skills; and finally, many programs actually help others. I have seen depressives and loners brighten up and become effective, creative leaders when given a Head Start class or a senior citizen to work with. Everyone likes to feel valuable and needed. Community-service programs meet this need and involve teenagers in their own education in a way that no other program can. They are also enormously cost-effective. Social agencies welcome the young "volunteers" and often provide supervision. What the school must do is make the commitment to the program, hire a coordinator, and provide transportation to the various service sites. I believe community service should be a requirement the same as any academic subject. Furthermore, the classes should be taught by professional, involved community leaders, social workers, neighborhood organizers, and the like. Teaching credentials should not be rigidly required; experience and competency should be prerequisites for the job. Put community service into the curriculum and everyone benefits.

Environmental Outdoor Studies

As we have noted in chapter one, our planet and hence our own human destiny are at risk as never before. It is conceivable that life—as we know it, and life as may be unique in all the cosmos—may come to an end by our own profligacy and improvidence. It is a real possibility. The fate of humankind and the very planet we live on will be determined by choices the next few generations will make. Consequently, familiarity, knowledge, and harmonic relationships between humans and the earth are essential. But, there is another kind of survival that environmental outdoor studies provide. This is the survival of the human spirit itself.

Anger and alienation are the dark side of the human spirit. They are rejections of life in its fullest. The hordes of angry and alienated students we see today are the products of an education which locks them up in confined, ugly classrooms, behind wire fences which surround asphalt fields that wrap around architecturally dull buildings, most of which are painted in marine green or a dull brown-yellow. After viewing one ugly campus after another, one has to wonder if there isn't some sort of conspiracy designed to make school as unattractive as possible. Then, within these overcrowded classrooms, some teachers try to teach of the beauty and preciousness of the earth. It cannot be done in such conditions. But take students to the mountains, the deserts, the oceans and lakes, and they come alive. They can walk, climb, hike—just being in the woods or on the beach engages them. They become active, and even the most disaffected cannot help but feel a sense of awe and mystery. Students who have never seen stars because of the city lights' reflections are amazed to see the infinity of stars and, at that moment, teachers can truly discuss with students the fragile place of our planet in the immensity of it all. To deny our urban children this outdoor experience is to deprive them of a joyous experience and thereby to contribute further to the anger and alienation from life which they feel and so disastrously express. Solution: put outdoor environmental programs and experiences into the curriculum.

Human Development

Finally, students come alive when they are allowed both to talk about their life's issues and to share their collective wisdom with each other. Life skills, human development, contemporary issues—whatever a school chooses to call them—are classes that not only engage students but that can lead to greater academic involvement and acquisition of skills. A student who will withdraw or intellectually drop out when asked to write about "the history of immigrants in New York" will often become drawn into research and writing when asked to write a history of his or her family. Once a given student writes such a short essay for a life studies class, he/she may then transfer the skills and techniques learned to a history assignment.

The issues students have to contend with today are not only immense and complex, but they cause such a level of fear and anxiety it is little wonder that many of them simply cannot study or do homework. But if they are given a place to talk, to make some sense of social issues, to be provided with the safety of a trained adult leading such discussions, then there is some possibility of dealing with and getting beyond their fears and anxieties. Public schools often react to a major crisis by bringing trained professionals into the schools to lead rap groups. This is all well and good, but it is putting salve on a wound rather than trying to prevent the wound in the first place. Schools across the land are torn apart by racial divisions and outright conflict, by sexual abuse at home and at school, by drugs-gangs-violence-rape, by teen pregnancies and suicides, and the list goes on. There must be a place for the young to deal with their daily assaults and deprivations—not just when a murder happens on campus. There are numerous models of such programs and classes available. What is needed first is the recognition that such classes are essential. What could we better spend our money achieving?

There can be no real learning without engagement. Disaffected, disaffiliated, disengaged students put in their time and soon drop out. Some drop out metaphorically and simply occupy space in classrooms, neither learning nor contributing, while others literally and in growing numbers just drop out of school. Often, they simply hang out on street corners and are easy prey for drug dealers and gang recruiters. They drop out of any meaningful possibility of gainful employment. Their prospects are miserable at best and then, of course, many wind up in the prison world. Once in the "prison complex," they are a huge financial drain on society and finally they *do* learn. In prison, they are engaged—in meanness, assaults, sadistic sexuality, criminal networking, in brutality and expanded antisocial values. The price we pay for our failure to educate properly is staggering. As a recent bumper sticker reads: "If you think education is expensive, try ignorance."

To put the arts, community service, outdoor environmental studies, and human development into our school curricula would certainly be costly. But we *can* afford to do so. *Not* to do so will cost us far more than we can afford.

Chapter 3

The Power of the Arts

We do not believe in ourselves until someone reveals that deep inside
us
something is valuable, worth listening to, worthy of our trust, sacred
to our touch.
Once we believe in ourselves, we can risk curiosity, wonder, spontane-
ous delight
or any experience that reveals the human spirit.

—e.e. cummings

Poetry is just the universe talking to itself
in a way that human beings can understand.

—Peter Levitt

In 1950, on receiving the Nobel Prize for Literature, William
Faulkner wrote of young writers who had "forgotten the problems' of the human heart in conflict with itself." If Faulkner
perceived such problems in 1950, what would he say today? At
least in 1950 young people were allowed into the arena where
these conflicts can be most profoundly experienced—that is,
the arts. As longtime music educator Herbert Zipper has
written:

> As much as we need the sciences to relate to outer reality, we need
> the arts to experience the spectrum of our mental responsiveness.
> The arts are primarily communications beyond the powers of verbal
> communication and as such are not replaceable by any other medi-
> ums. Each art is opening its own door toward the realization of our
> capacity to feel, to think and to recognize. As we begin to learn in
> early childhood how to communicate verbally, we must begin in early
> childhood to learn how the arts are communicating with us. If we

deprive children of this learning process, we are perpetrating grand
larceny on generations. (letter to author, 1988)

In 1965, the *Rockefeller Panel Report* on the arts asked a question that was not only real then but which shows how much further conditions have deteriorated since 1965: "For the school to make sure that a child attends a concert, a play, or a dance recital once a year for ten years will neither allow the child to acquire a habit nor create a sense of necessity about art. These pleasures will remain something to take or leave, and the chances are on the side of the latter. But to provide live performances for young people with sufficient frequency, quality, and range to establish a lifelong habit is generally impossible within the context of American education at the present time. Is there any chance that this context can be changed? And if so, how?" At that time, the panel was concerned about children attending a concert, play, or dance recital *only once a year*. Today, in public schools all across the country, they attend virtually *none*.

The importance of the arts in education has been given strong testimony by any number of studies, ranging from the Rockefeller Panel in 1965 to innumerable contemporary governmental studies. Everyone seems to agree. Nevertheless, they are still the first to be subject to budgetary evisceration. As a nation we proclaim their importance, feel virtuous in doing so, and then—with a tsk-tsk—we watch them cut with sad acknowledgments. "Well, too bad, but it had to be." This is the pattern.

Educators try to explain the doom and disgrace which these cuts and this attitude toward the arts create. Yet little is done. Occasional conferences, calls for new standards and curriculum revisions occur but only as Band-Aids, never as the result of a massive reordering of national priorities. Yet, does anyone doubt that such a reordering is essential?

My argument? It is simple: the arts have the power to transform society. The arts do all the things writers have attested for the well-being of every individual, but they have a magic beyond that. The results are far greater than the sum of the parts. A nation in love with creativity would not have allowed itself to sell an entire generation of children down the drain. The trillions of dollars spent on erecting missiles could have engaged millions of schoolchildren in creative self-expression rather than the gangs/drugs/sex/violence pattern—the result of neglect and deprivation.

We spend an average of $5,000 per pupil per year (K–12). We spend $25,000 per prisoner per year. A few hundred additional dollars per pupil to restore the arts to every schoolchild would save thousands in the long run. Children who believe in themselves can risk creative forms of self-expression; they do not need to kill, to spawn neglected children, to join gangs, to drop out, to anesthetize themselves to life through drugs. They can take pleasure in bringing artistic projects to life instead of taking life away from life.

A Pragmatic Appeal

I believe in all the arguments in favor of the arts, but rather than dwell on the philosophical or aesthetic apologies for the arts, I offer instead this pragmatic appeal. Every dollar invested in arts education for children will save us hundreds of thousands of dollars later on. Restore the arts to the curriculum today and tomorrow you receive returns of fewer dropouts, fewer criminals, less taxes to support the prison system, safer streets. And, not the least of the list, you receive the creative contributions—paintings, musical compositions, theatrical productions, dance recitals—of young people loving life rather than hating *you* (the power structure). Only fools would pass up this investment opportunity. Yet, as a society, this foolishness is exactly what we have done. We have taken out of the curriculum those experiences, those activities (note the roots *act, active*), and those programs which actively *engage* young people and connect them to the life force. Instead, we stuff them into overcrowded schools and then turn them out onto the streets where the pimps, drug dealers, gang recruiters, child-pornography promoters, and garden-variety purveyors of vulgar materialism *engage* the young. Don't pay the art teacher to promote the arts; allow the gang recruiters and drug dealers an uncontested arena for promotion and enrollment. The idiocy and meanness of this sin of omission is far worse than the sins of commission by our young. We know better; they do not. We deprive them of our wisdom and knowledge and this neglect deprives them of a decent life.

The arts cannot solve all the problems of our society, but they have a disproportionate power to transform and inspire. A child who is allowed the thrill of making a mask or choreographing a simple movement is being allowed to say, "I matter," "I have value." Feeling so, he/she can then enter a math class capable of thinking more clearly or writing an essay with more confidence. Everything takes on a different perspective when you think you matter. The arts are the arena wherein students can most quickly and directly make a personal statement. Solving $2x + 2y = 10$ can be satisfying, but for many students it is not the same experience as writing a poem, making a song, or drawing a self-portrait. These are personal expressions which allow the creator to feel a sense of individuality and unique individual worth. Individuals do not need to join gangs and attack innocent citizens on the streets. They know the joys of creation; they do not need the indulgence of destruction.

There is yet another societal and pragmatic reason for placing the arts back in the center of the curriculum. As our culture and country give evidence of falling apart—that is, of becoming a nation of distinct and separate ethnic, racial, and class groups, hostile and disconnected—the arts can play a healing and unifying role.

> Moreover, in our era of acute scrutiny and self-consciousness when so much attention is focused on multiculturalism, cultural diversity, gender issues, and ethnic identity, the role of art should be recognized and elevated to the status of a *must* in the curriculum. Consider what the making and the study of art is about: a nonverbal connection with every culture in history, independent of a chronological, linear progression through the centuries. Art can help young people feel connected with virtually all ethnic groups and with all religions and beliefs. It helps them understand the way other people look and looked, live and lived, and the rituals and pageants of their cultures—an array of events from wars to betrothals, from family portraits to bestiaries, from objects and images of pure fantasy to the simplicity of two apples in a bowl, from apocalyptic visions of heaven and hell to images of love and fear and hope. In short, students exposed to making art and studying the various dimensions of art can enter a world of direct experience with the entire human race. There is no better or clearer way to understand the differences and similarities of our diverse world and history. (Lehrer, 1994: 5)

Physical differences do not define our humanness, our individual souls. Obvious differences divide people and these divisions can lead to violence. Through the arts, we can penetrate beyond superficiality where not only interesting and life-affirming differences reside, but where commonality can also be discovered. Superficial differences are walls but as Robert Frost wrote, "before I build a wall I'd ask to know what I was walling in or walling out." The arts break down walls. Often, they do not rely on language or objective measurement, but instead they appeal to human emotions, to the five senses, to intuition and subjective ways of knowing. Without these *skills* we are ultimately lost.

There seems to be, however, a growing apprehension on the part of the American people that *something is wrong*; that our children are growing up lacking certain sensitivities and goals that the previous generation values. While the causes are many, one is clear: we are denying them a fundamental and humanly imperative need—that of self-expression in the arts.

To compound our problems, the United States is experiencing perhaps the most dramatic demographic transformation of any country in mankind's history. This is an extraordinary statement. Such a reality obviously contains within it the potential for unimaginable violence and conflict. It is also a glorious opportunity. The opportunity is to create a rich tapestry from culturally and historically diverse threads. Instead of violence and division, we could consciously seek to celebrate our different heritages and to create from those differences a new, agreed-upon story, a new national identity, an identity which does not obliterate any one story but gathers them together into a new collaborative story. And in this process the ARTS will be essential. They will be the celebratory expressions of that new story. They—the ARTS—will be both process and product. Without them, I fear, we will be lost. One can hardly avoid repeating what has been said so often: "the ARTS are not a frill, not extracurricular; they are essential to our students' lives and to our society's well-being: essential, not tangential; essential.

Twelve Arguments for the Arts

In an arts advocacy article (why is it that in America the arts so often need advocates when in other nations the value of the arts is clear to all), the author, William Cleveland, provided six arguments in support of the arts in America. They are worth summarizing for those who like clear lists:

1.   The arts help us communicate about transcendent values and issues: Indeed, the arts speak to levels of human consciousness in unique ways which only they can reach. Without the arts in our curriculum, we deprive children of a deep human need: the need to explore mystery (Cleveland, 1992: 86);

2.   The arts are a basic educational reform: There are many different kinds of intelligences, and the arts offer an alternative for success and respectability for students who may not do as well in other subjects (86);

3.   The arts provide a common language in a complex global culture: The arts build bridges between radically different cultures and language groups (87);

4.   The arts help maintain our competitiveness in a technological age: Artists are innovators. The roles of the artist and the technological innovator are often interchangeable. In his book, *The Paradox of the Silicon Savior*, Grant Venerable (1988: 87) points out "that the very best engineers and technical designers (in the Silicon Valley) are, nearly without exception, practicing musicians";

5.   The arts are a proven strategy for healing, prevention, and empowerment: This assertion is almost self-explanatory. In case study after study, the arts are shown "to be an effective and cost-beneficial resource for reducing violence, recidivism, and psychopathology" (88);

6.   The arts are an essential resource for community development: they provide jobs, encourage tourism, attract audiences. "Recent research shows that each dollar spent on the arts generates three to four dollars in non-arts expenditures" (86).

To Cleveland's list of six, I would add a few others:

7.   Programs in the arts can radically improve graduation rates, grades, and overall achievement levels: This has been demonstrated in report after study after conference (*U.S. News and World Report*, March 30, 1992: 52–54);

8.   The arts teach skills needed in the twenty-first century workforce: The capacity for working in teams, creative thinking, self-esteem, imagination, invention. All are the province of the arts;

9.   The arts develop leadership: In every artistic endeavor the best artists are pushing the boundaries of human knowledge, expanding the breadth and understanding of human experience, and creating for the world something that was not there before. We bemoan our lack of leadership in politics and education today and yet we cut from the curriculum this important arena for developing leaders. It makes no sense.

10.   The arts inspire self-confidence and help keep kids interested in school: My own experience has shown that often a recorder class or a painting class is *the* class which keeps a student coming to school instead of dropping out and then becoming an at-risk student, some of whom inevitably join the prison culture rather than the culture at large;

11.   The arts help energize the school environment: Paintings in the halls, murals on the walls, music assemblies, recorder and song at ceremonies, plays and dance recitals—all breathe life into a school. In the past few years, I have watched the arts lift the morale of several entire schools—principals, teachers, parents, as well as students;

12.   The arts are a crucial way to honor and celebrate the earth: If we accept the argument of Thomas Berry and Miriam McGillis (see chapter 7 of this book) that our main purpose as humans is to celebrate our emergence as the beings in which the earth becomes conscious of itself, then the arts are the *primary* means by which we celebrate this process.

I conclude this chapter on the power of the arts with two quotes: one from Ernest Fleishmann, executive vice president and Managing Director of the Los Angeles Philharmonic, and the other from the late author, Katherine Ann Porter.

> History does not measure a nation's greatness by its corporate balance sheets, or even by its military bands. It is to the writers, the musicians, the philosophers, the painters and sculptors, the builders of the great cathedrals that we look for inspiration, for the impetus to create and go forward to make a positive impact on the world's civilization. If, however, we follow the dictates of the anti-arts brigade in Congress, the impact of the United States on the cultural progress of our world will be one of shame and sorrow, of guns and jails, and bottom lines.
>
> —Ernest Fleishmann

The arts live continuously, and they live literally by faith; their nature and their shapes and their uses survive unchanged in all that matters through times of interruption, diminishment, neglect; they outlive governments and creeds and societies, even the very civilizations that produced them. They cannot be destroyed altogether because they represent the substance of faith and the only reality. They are what we find again when the ruins are cleared away.

—Katherine Ann Porter

Chapter 4

Mysteries: Education for Hope and Community

There are moments—very rare ones—when one sees, hears, and understands on a level that does not correspond to everyday life, on a level that surpasses in intensity that with which our senses have acquainted us. Almost as if the vibrations—either too slow or too quick—that escape our perception suddenly became noticeable. On these occasions we are left . . . almost breathless. . . . We enter a kind of interior silence like that of a blank page, ready to receive a word that cannot be foreseen.

> —Victoria Ocampo, "The Forest" (translated by Doris Meyer from *TESTIMONIOS VII*, 1965)

We know the truth, not only
    by reason, but by the heart.

> —Blaise Pascal

What has been developed at Crossroads School is a significant educational innovation and, given the spiritual crisis of our society, Mysteries should become a model for similar programs at every level of the educational system.

> —John Broomfield, former president of the California Institute of Integral Studies

She walked boldly into my office, a twelfth-grade student, said, "May I talk?" and almost without waiting for my invitation, said, "Tomorrow, tomorrow, tomorrow—that's all you adults ever talk about. When do we get to enjoy today?" She went on to say that all she heard of was preparing for tomorrow's quiz, next month's SATs, the April college acceptance dates, college majors and choice of vocation—even where she might ultimately settle down, but never about today's dreams and fears and personal complexities. Then abruptly, she got up and left—feeling, I suppose, slightly better for at least having had the opportunity to vent and be heard.

I, however, felt depressed and thought about her feelings for several days. Then I had coffee with my friend and mentor, Jack Zimmerman—an extraordinary educational visionary—who said, "Well, why don't you do something about it?" And he then explained "council" to me.

Council is an ancient practice emanating from the Native American traditions. It was a practice which Jack had introduced earlier at a school he helped to create named Heartlight. The school did not survive for financial reasons, he explained, but the practice of council was a great success. I left our meeting exhilarated: here was a way to address the concerns of the girl who came to see me; here was a way, I was soon to discover, to deal directly with anger and alienation.

The Council Process

The council process begins with a circle. The students usually sit on the floor, with someone, often the adult facilitator, acting as the one in charge of moving things along. The lights may be dimmed and a candle lit in the center of the circle to imbue the whole process with a sense of seriousness and ceremony. The group will also select a "talking piece"—it might be a gourd, or a small stone, or a special wand or rattle—that is held by the speaker and that one must be holding to speak. Thus, each person in the circle has a chance to speak, uninterrupted, and each person must *listen* to others without speaking. The rules of council are simple: (1) speak from the heart; (2) listen from the heart; (3) be lean and concise. One is also allowed to simply pass the talking piece without speaking. In fact, silence often communicates in a powerful way. The leader of the given council will also stress the importance of confidentiality: that what is said in council is sacred and must not be repeated to others outside of council. In fifteen years of this program at Crossroads, the students have honored this principle with remarkable integrity and loyalty. Rarely has a student's trust been violated by another student. I believe the students are so grateful to receive the trust we place in them that they would not consider jeopardizing the program by betraying that trust. Council—on a given day—may or may not have a specific theme. Some days students will simply go around the circle giving "a weather report," that is, talking about how they are feeling and dealing with life at that time in their lives. Or a council may focus on a topic such as death, divorce, the break-up of friendships, social pressure, or any other theme which may emerge from the group.

Armed with this beginner's understanding of council, and with Jack Zimmerman's promise to help launch the program, I decided to waste no time. With Jack as facilitator, we began several councils of fourteen to sixteen seniors each. We decided right off the bat to give the class a special name—"Mysteries"—since this would be much of its subject matter. These years—from twelve to eighteen—are times of profound changes, questioning, confusion, and mystery. Their bodies are changing; their feelings toward their parents, their friends, and themselves are changing; their moral compasses are in wild fluctuation, with emotions of love and hate existing almost simultaneously. They are starting to form a sense of identity, but it is fragile and insecure, and all of this is happening so fast it is a huge mystery to them. If we help them make some sense of it all, it helps not only their inner world, it even helps with their academics.

When we launched the class, I anticipated different reactions from three groups in the school: the parents would be hostile, the teachers would welcome it, and the students would resent *yet another program* in their busy lives. I was wrong on all three counts. The parents—almost from day one—loved the program. Their children were coming home and initiating discussions about friendship, respect, listening, the complexities of modern living, and so on. If the parent had tried to initiate such discussions, the adolescents would clam up, but not so when they initiated topics. The faculty were frightened and resistant—in part because they resented the intrusion of a new program in the schedule, and in part because they were afraid students would "discuss" them in the council circles. The students embraced the program almost from the very beginning and their only complaint was that we waited until their senior year to provide such a program.

Responding to Parent Concerns

Initially, concerns were expressed by a few parents: was this a touchie-feelie program? Was it group therapy? Was it an encounter group? Was it a quasi-religious gathering? I met with groups of parents and answered questions. No, I explained, regarding all four concerns. One, there is no touching at all in council. Two, because each individual speaks as an individual and because there is no specific response by the leader/facilitator or the group to anyone, there is no therapy involved in council. It is, I suppose, true that speaking from the heart about one's life is somewhat therapeutic, but the focus of the group is not problem-solving for any individual. Three, for the same reasons it is not an encounter group—there is simply no focus on any one person, nor is combativeness or rudeness permitted by the facilitator. (On occasion, the facilitator may speak out of turn to intervene should a given student go beyond the rules—but this is quite rare.) And fourth, there is no dogma or religious content to the circles. Students simply speak from their individual hearts about what they feel impelled to share. The only ceremonial ritual involved is lighting a candle. "The candle," explains Zimmerman, "is seen as asking for guidance and light . . . it changes the environment . . . it's like when you start a story with *once upon a time*. It shifts consciousness." Once parents heard this, they were reassured and, over the years they have praised and thanked the school for this unique program.

Launched for seniors in 1984, the program was such a success that it was soon added at grades seven and eight, then grades nine through eleven, and later at kindergarten through sixth grade. Thus, the whole school now "practices" council, and by the time students graduate, I believe they have gained "listening skills," a greater sense of awareness of others, and a great sense of self-awareness. I have had college admissions offices and interviewers say over and over that they can pick Crossroads students out of any group of high school applicant's— that they have a certain self-confidence and openness which is not the norm. And, if knowledge of how to function in community and self-knowledge are two forms of intelligence (they are two of Howard Gardner's "seven kinds of intelligence"), then Mysteries is a clear curricular way of developing these two "intelligences." Most people do not do poorly in life because they cannot read or calculate theorems or sing or dance; they do poorly because they cannot listen to others, they cannot work well in a group, they do not perceive how they are perceived by others, they do not know their own limitations. Mysteries classes or council address all of these areas and help young people learn how to function well in each of these areas. It should not be considered, as extracurricula as a frill, or add-on, or as a luxury class. I can only be grateful to the girl who walked unannounced into my office ten years ago and helped me see the light.

Since that time, the Mysteries program has not only grown and flourished at Crossroads School, it has spread to other private *and* public schools. One expansion occurred in conjunction with Crossroads School and came from a council of public and private school administrators (which we call "The New Visions II" group). One public school vice-principal, Lana Brody, of Palms Middle School, reports that this council of colleagues has been "the most stimulating, dream-fulfilling experience I have had. I can share dreams, which to public-school peers would seem naive, and feel I'm understood." The story of bringing council to Palms was featured by a Los Angeles freelance writer, Kathy Seal, in the Pacific Southwest Airlines magazine, *Spirit*:

> Thus Brody felt comfortable enough at a New Visions II meeting about eight weeks before the L.A. riots to voice her fears of an increasingly tense climate at Palms. The well-respected magnet school, like many others in Los Angeles, has a global admixture of students speaking more than thirty different native languages. This spring, a few typical early adolescent conflicts—taunting remarks, a fistfight—had taken on non-typical racial overtones. Brody remembers feeling sad, and not knowing what to do with her fear.
>
> The assistant principal was worried about what she saw happening, events that she now realized were preliminaries to the L.A. riots. It was almost an ominous foreboding that you could smell or touch or feel."
>
> Brody wanted some kind of program for Palms that would break down stereotypical thinking among the students. "I wanted something . . . that would imbue kids with the proper ethics and understanding they'd need to build the bridges that would be necessary in their adult lives in this city," she says.
>
> Cummins and Zimmerman suggested forming a "council" of student-body officers and other student leaders at Palms. For the past

ten years, Crossroads and several other private schools in southern California have used such groups as part of a "Mysteries," or human-development program.

One such session last April found Zimmerman sitting cross-legged on a classroom floor in a circle with teacher Sylvia Thomas and ten kids from a variety of ethnic backgrounds, including African, Japanese, Jewish, Mexican, Korean, Filipino, Chinese, Vietnamese, and Arab. A candle burned in the circle's center. It was the eve of the jury decision in the second Rodney King beating trial, and Zimmerman asked the kids to give a "weather report" on how they'd feel as an L.A. City Council member on this day. One boy was sprawled on the floor, chin cupped in his left palm and elbow on the floor. Another rested his head on his arms, which were folded on the corner of the teacher's desk. A girl on the rug fidgeted with a pencil, and picked at her fingernails with a teenager's nervous energy. All listened quietly as each spoke, one by one, of their confusion, tension, and anger. (Seale, 1993)

After adding the program at grade eight, the Palms Middle School administration was so delighted that they expanded it to the entire school. Now, other public schools have asked Palms how they might launch such a program. Several private schools in California and in other states have launched similar programs.

Addressing Student Needs

What need, one might ask, does this kind of program address? Is it truly a *need*, or is it an educational *wish* that is of less importance than other fundamental needs? I would argue that it is the former—a *need*. Young people today live in times in which the fear of nuclear annihilation has given way to new anxieties—fear of environmental degradation, toxicity, and even extinction, fear of strange and new diseases, fear of not finding a job, fear of violence in the streets and neighborhoods, and the vague fears of living meaningless lives. Although writing in the 1950s of the previous nuclear fear, William Faulkner's words ring true in today's new world:

. . . There are no longer problems of the spirit. There is only the question: when will I be blown up? Because of this, the young man or woman writing today has forgotten the problems of the human heart in conflict with itself. . . . He [she] must learn them again. He [she] must teach himself that the basest of things is to be afraid; and, teaching [her]self that, forget it forever, leaving no room in his workshop for anything but the old verities and truths of the heart, the old universal truths lacking which any story is ephemeral and doomed—love and honor and pity and pride and compassion and sacrifice. (Faulkner, 1950: 723–724)

These truths and these stories can find a place for expression in council. It is a place where the young, in a setting of trust and confidentiality, can express their fears and speak of their hopes and dreams, their verities and truths. This is not a wish—this is a deep human need.

When students have a time and place to tell their stories, many wonderful results occur. Students learn to be more careful in forming quick judgments of others. Often, they will sit "in council" with students they had written off years ago as geeks or wierdos or jerks, but in council, they will learn that these students have similar fears and rich interior worlds. They listen to each other and they learn. New friendships are formed. Old prejudgements (prejudices) are discarded. Furthermore, boys—who are *not* encouraged by our macho-saturated culture to acknowledge or express emotions—in council learn to express, and to hear, feelings. They learn that it is not unmanly to share their inner world with others. It is a great gift that boys receive in these sessions.

Dealing with Stress

In addition to these virtues, Mysteries helps address another issue. Shelly Kessler, a former chair of the human development and mysteries programs at Crossroads, writes, "until now we have defined the problem [in the American youth culture] primarily in terms of the 'losers'—high school drop-outs, drug abusers, suicide victims, and pregnant teens. But the emptiness and fear are not only the afflictions of the apathetic or despairing. . . . What we hear, see, smell, and taste in the atmosphere of our best schools is *stress*. Too little time and too much work to do. . . . There is no time left for play. No time for daydreaming . . ." (Kessler, 1990: 12). Council, however, can be a place where these various stresses are shared, discussed, and in some cases, alleviated. When faculty members participate in councils, they come to see the school day and the lives of individual students in a different light. Ideally, I would have every teacher sit in on one mysteries class each year. It would help teachers see the life issues which their students are struggling to comprehend and it would help teachers learn to listen. Teachers, like all adults who deal with the young, are better talkers than listeners. The Mysteries Program focuses on the students. As Kessler writes, the program "listens and responds to the voices from the other side of the report card."

> I'm scared of growing up too fast. One night I cried about it and I was uncertain about the seventh grade. My parents love me a lot and I am happy, but I'm scared. What can I do?
>
> —a seventh-grader

> How far with self-confidence and contentment can I go before I reach selfishness? I always want to be better than everyone else, and I know that's wrong. I never want to be average and I like to believe everyone else is. That's bad. Can I be a special person and be happy and still not think I'm above everyone else?
>
> —a sophomore

> Why do people want to destroy each other? What is it about human nature that prohibits us from trusting each other? Why is it such a sin to be vulnerable?
>
> —a senior

Why is it a sin to be vulnerable? this high school student asks with wisdom. The answer I would offer is that being vulnerable, being open to others, sharing ideas and feelings with kindness and humility is a profound human achievement. As poet Peter Levitt states, "sin is alienation from the self; it is the distance between wholeness and hollowness." Mysteries classes and the council format are not some sort of miracle cure, but they do help to counteract the materialism, egoism, racial and class divisiveness, and the frantic sense of despair and meaninglessness which our young (and older) people are feeling (Crossroads, 1990; Zimmerman, 1996). Conflict, anger, bigotry, and selfishness are all the result of people living alone with their fears and anxieties and, consequently, living apart from community. Council teaches us how to live *in community*.

Chapter 5

The New Social Studies, Part I: Global Issues

You were born for one reason, and so was I.
We were born to save the creation.

—Helen Caldicott

Soon all of us will sleep under the earth,
we who never let each other sleep above it.

—Marina Tsvetaeva

History is a study of the past. At best, it is a leisurely exploration of crevices and byways, and obscure caverns and quays.
Often, its fascination is to be found in human eccentricities
and curiosities. I would hope this quality of history study is
never lost, but I would argue that our schools and teachers
now need to be united in facing a new, unprecedented, and
indescribably urgent call to action—the preservation of the
planet. And, I would argue, history/social studies/humanities
teachers must be part of heeding this call. (Throughout this
chapter, I will simply use the term "history" to represent
classes/courses which are sometimes called social studies, humanities, world cultures, and the like) History, is fascinating;
it is true. However, the planet itself faces desperate conditions
and impending choices, and the succeeding generations which
will need to confront these conditions and make these choices
must be armed with the knowledge of how these conditions
came to be and what consequences might logically be expected
to flow from decision A or B. History cannot predict, nor can
knowledge of it guarantee against repetition. It can, however,
provide a basis for intelligent decision-making and for under-

standing trends and possibilities. So, we must first identify the forces which appear to be threatening our very survival and begin our history-curriculum discussions by studying their evolution and examining humankind's attempts—conscious or otherwise—to deal with them. Survival and a decent life for all peoples are not someone else's issues. They are everyone's, and in education they must be placed at the center of the curricula.

What then are these issues? I believe there are *three* overriding issues:

- Overpopulation
- Environmental destruction
- Political/economic/social/cultural disparity

The three are intertwined and interrelated; they cut across traditional lines of inquiry, and the crisis they pose together is a relatively recent phenomenon in history which is growing in exponential leaps and bounds. Thus, a new history curriculum should have at its center the goal of teaching students how humankind might seek an equitable, sustainable planet.

To combine those three principles in one statement: the survival of the planet depends upon gaining immediate control of the world's population, curtailing environmental destruction, and designing a system of world government and federations of nations to correct the disparity of the world's wealth and to achieve a more equitable distribution of the world's resources among nations, regions, and individuals. Simply put, there must be fewer people, less ecological destruction, and greater fairness. Otherwise, at the rate we are going, overpopulation will lead to further mass starvation, overtaxing of the world's resources, and inevitably, revolution and anarchy as the poor become more and more desperate. Clearly, the planet cannot sustain the population which now exists, and nearly *doubling* the population in the next twenty-five years will cause calamities on every front—social, political, economic, and cultural. The erosion of the earth's soils and the massive problems of waste removal spell self-destruction; the fouling of water and air, and the elimination of the earth's rain forests spell self-destruction; global warming and the depletion of the ozone layer and the wholesale extinction of species spell self-destruction. And soon. Each school, department, and individual teacher, I believe, must redirect their efforts toward addressing these issues. The study of history is one place where we may begin. Today's students are tomorrow's managers and leaders and they will *lead* only to the degree that they are aware of these deeper issues and have developed the values and commitment to bring about change in the world.

This trilogy—world population, the environment, and social justice—if placed at the center of not only the history curriculum, but at the center of the entire curriculum, would truly prepare students for the challenges and realities of the emerging twenty-first century. Thus, world population studies would, of necessity, require students to learn about geography and anthropology. For teachers and departments willing to tackle such issues, there are wonderful texts and papers available from the Worldwatch Institute. Each year, the institute publishes a *State of the World* series of essays on topics dealing with the earth's environment. It would be a superb text for high school and college students. The institute also publishes excellent papers on topics such as air pollution, soil erosion, water conservation, reforesting the earth, global warming, and the like.

Investigating Global Issues Across the Curriculum

Any efforts the world and its future leaders may undertake to control the exploding population patterns will surely require knowledge of the cultural, religious, and social practices of peoples everywhere—particularly in the less-educated parts of the world where the population increases are most severe. Math classes, beginning in the elementary years, rather than dealing with hypothetical, statistical, and word problems of apples and oranges or widgets might deal with real issues of demographics, population shifts, birth rates, and the like. Certainly, any study of world populations will lead directly to human biology, nutrition, genetics, and other sciences. In addition, issues of economics, politics, and international relations will be essential for discussions of population control.

The world's population is perhaps the single most important factor in mankind's newly conceived quest for an environmentally sustainable planet. When I graduated from college in 1959, I had never heard the word or concept of ecology discussed. Rachel Carson's *The Sea Around Us* was published in 1961. In the three decades since then, we have come to learn that we humans are in a life and death race with devastation—a race of our own making. We have only recently come to see that the earth and its surrounding biosphere may not support the disastrous population increases which are occurring at this moment in history. It took from the dawn of humanity until 1830 for the first billion people to inhabit the earth. The second billion took only one hundred years—from 1830 to 1930. Three billion more arrived by 1990. The next billion will take only eleven years. We are adding the equivalent of a New York City every month to planet earth. As Paul Kennedy writes: "The earth is under a twofold attack from human beings—the excessive demands and wasteful habits of affluent populations of developed countries and the billions of new mouths born in the developing world who (very naturally) aspire to increase their own consumption levels" (Kennedy, 1994: 31).

By now, just about every educated person in America is aware, to some degree, of the threats to our environment. It is as though all of recorded history has gathered into one ecological bomb which is threatening to explode in our historical instant. I remember as a child hearing the expression that "X or Y was about as useless as spitting in the ocean." The mentality then was that the ocean is limitless—an infinite reservoir of life; an unpollutable mass. But now we are learning, in a tragically slow manner, that the world's oceans are finite and precious. According to the Worldwatch Institute, the world's oceans have been nearly fished to the limits. And, if current mismanagement continues, we can expect a future in which millions of fishers are out of work . . . a future in which traditional fishing cultures from Nova Scotia to Malaysia will disappear. Not only are the once abundant north Atlantic cod now almost commercially extinct; not only are the western Atlantic bluefin tuna down to only 10 percent of their former abundance; not only are several north Pacific salmon species on the brink of extinction, and oysters in the Chesapeake Bay at only *4 percent* of former levels; but all this loss of jobs and resources is occurring as the population continues relentlessly to grow (Weber, 1994: 23).

The Urgency in Dealing with Global Issues

The earth is a tiny jewel poised precariously in the immensity of space and is dependent upon limited resources which are dying out daily. Because of the rate at which these resources are being exploited and eliminated, we cannot afford the luxury of leaving it to the next generation or the next century to solve the problems. An extinct species is a problem that cannot be solved. The schools today must add a note of urgency to their own curriculum planning and must be leaders in raising consciousness and resolve among the young. So, to the study of world populations must be added the interrelated study of the environment. Traditional courses (chemistry, physics, biology, geology, oceanography, ecology) which are currently in the curriculum may remain but they must provide a different focus. Chemistry, for example, might add units on the effects and availability of plutonium and highly enriched uranium and how mankind can clean up after the arms race. In short, our students need to gain eco-literacy. And, in all of this, existing computer studies programs at the elementary and high school level will take on added importance as issues become more complex and as information proliferates *and* becomes accessible. It is important to note that while the word *environment* has become politicized for many, the long-term issues transcend politics. Responsible citizens and politicians alike see this clearly and avoid mindless name-calling. Survival is not a liberal or a conservative cause; it is simple human sanity.

It is crucial, in addition, that schools across the land study issues of social justice. One problem, stated quite simply, is that the few control most of the world's wealth. To illustrate, the net worth of 350 billionaires is equal to that of 45 percent of the world's population—and the gap is widening. Meanwhile, the many experience deprivation ranging from the merely inconvenient and irksome all the way to degradation, starvation, and despair beyond telling. Most of the "haves" would prefer not to speak of it, let alone deal with it. Yet, it is this very disparity which threatens to destroy us all—the haves and have-nots alike. The harmful rays of sunlight pouring through hole(s) in the ozone layer will descend upon the rich and poor alike. Certainly the issue of how to preserve the ozone layer is important to study in science classes as well as civics and current events classes. Whether one is an idealist or a self-interested "have," the preservation of the planet will require not only controlling and reducing current birth rates around the world—a daunting task—but will require a more equitable distribution of the world's wealth—or else. Or else what? Or else, for example, the have-nots will destroy every acre of rain forest, will migrate by the millions, will wage wars of desperation. The problem does not stop here, for even if the have-nots do acquire some of the blessings of technology and materialism, then they will simply inflate the amount of air pollution, waste and garbage, and so on, which the haves *now* inflict upon the globe.

The challenge for history and social studies teachers and for schools is not only to study the problems, but to seek sources of solutions; to bring speakers onto campuses who have offbeat and inspiring ideas about the future, visionaries, futurists, dreamers. Young people need now more than ever to be inspired, to be infused with a sense of the possible, of hope. They need to read books (see the Reference List and Further Reading at the back of this book) envisioning a new world. A story, perhaps apocryphal, but perhaps not, has it that a woman once asked Albert Einstein what he would recommend for her young child to read so that the child would become as brilliant as Einstein. "Fairy tales," he replied. "And then what?" she asked. "More fairy tales," he replied. TV news, movies, newspapers are all filled either with trivia, or with doom and gloom. Reality for much of our youth is equally depressing. Youth should be a time of dreaming about the future, of making grandiose plans, of wild idealism. In addition to studying the environmental crises, schools and teachers can help restore a sense of hope for the future. Science fiction, fantasy, utopian novels, and the study of actual historical utopian communities should be added to the curriculum. Students can then use these as a basis for designing their own twenty-first and twenty-second century utopias, model cities, new federations of nations, and the like. Dreaming needs to be encouraged and nurtured.

In our new social studies classes, we must educate a generation of future leaders who are more knowledgeable and conscious, less selfish, and more concerned about posterity than the previous generations which created our current mess. One thing we *cannot* do is to defer the problems to yet another future generation hoping to squeeze just one more decade or half-century's blessings (i.e., profits) out of the wounded and dying earth, and to continue to ignore the unspeakable misery of the poor and wretched of the earth.

Chapter 6

The New Social Studies, Part II: American Issues

Difference need not, but can, be a tremendous
barrier between people, and there are few ways
of breaching it other than through democracy
itself.

—Anne Phillips, *Democracy and Difference*

There must be a passion to end poverty,
for nothing less than that will do.

—Michael Harrington

The three overriding global issues of overpopulation, environmental degradation, and social injustice are equally critical in America. If each school were properly addressing them, these issues would inform and give focus to the entire curricula—not just social studies. Certainly these three issues call upon science and math and foreign languages for ways of studying and addressing the problems. Certainly in history and social studies classes the issues may receive particularly close scrutiny. If our very survival depends upon reversing current trends—this is a hypothesis we would now (given the enormous body of evidence) be crazy not to consider—then the trends must be studied as a prelude to change. A new generation of informed leaders must be educated. Thus, when we consider American history classes or American studies (or social studies), we need to look at those forces which are most directly threatening to destroy our social and national fabric. I believe they *can* be identified, isolated for purposes of study, analyzed, and ultimately—if we find the national will—changed. Each of these forces is enormously complex and is the subject of voluminous research and study, but they must be confronted or else. As W. H. Auden wrote in the poem "September 1, 1939," "We must love one another or die." Though inevitably we all do die, while we have life we must seek solutions to ultimate problems or risk dying unnecessarily before the final necessary death—not only individually, but collectively. Spiritual apathy, poverty, segregation and racism, decay and violence in our cities are all a kind of death—figuratively as well as literally. So I would argue that our history and social studies curricula should look at four current phenomena and then ask, "How did these come about?" This would be more than a year's course; it is, in fact, a lifetime's study. But it is necessary to begin. The four are:

- spiritual drift and confusion;
- a growing disparity of wealth;
- *dis*integration of society;
- the breaking down of cities.

These four are a subset of the larger issue of social justice but, as we saw with the three global issues discussed in chapter 5, these four are interrelated and are all a result of a failure of priorities, values, and the national will. For this reason, I list spiritual drift and confusion as the first and foremost issue to address. A nation whose values were properly sorted out would not allow the rate of homicide, child abuse, homelessness, poverty, and urban decay that we now permit.

Spiritual Drift, Confusion, and Apathy

In 1950, upon receiving the Nobel Prize for Literature, William Faulker wrote:

> I decline to accept the end of man. It is easy enough to say that man is immortal simply because he will endure: that when the last ding-dong of doom has clanged and faded from the last worthless rock hanging tideless in the last red and dying evening, that even then there will still be one more sound: that of his puny inexhaustible voice, still talking. I refuse to accept this. I believe that man will not merely endure: he will prevail. He is immortal, not because he alone among

creatures has an inexhaustible voice, but because he has a soul, a spirit capable of compassion and sacrifice and endurance.

Upon first hearing these words, I, like many of my contemporaries, was stirred and inspired. While I still believe in their underlying sentiment, I now feel differently. I can now see an "end to man." I can see what Robinson Jeffers meant when speaking of man as a stain upon the earth, a stain which someday will be removed so that the land can return to those who live in harmony with it—that is, hawks and deer and sea creatures. Young people today have little sense of posterity or hope for a bright future. Progress is no longer a blind faith; rather self-aggrandizement is more the fare of the day. Young people today are aware that their parents' generation has for the first time in our nation's history bequeathed to them *less* than those adults received when they were young: fewer healthy cities, less clean air and water, a national debt of staggering proportions, less safety in the streets, seemingly less honesty in politics, less fairness in society and, hence, smoldering rage in the ghettos and elsewhere in the society. How can a young person, therefore, look to the future with confidence? Young people today know that presidents sometimes lie; they know that leaders send young people to fight and die in wars that they acknowledge later they were aware were wrong even as they sent them; they know that elections can be bought and that their leaders know all of this but do not care so long as they can find ways to get reelected. Is it any wonder, therefore, that the young become cynical, despairing, and ultimately selfish and apathetic? As David M. Kennedy (former President of Stanford University) recently wrote, "Democracy . . . cannot easily survive in an atmosphere of cynical and contemptuous regard for government itself." The problems seem so immense and so neglected that many say "To hell with it, I'll get what I can for me." What then is the way out of this darkness (1995: M3)?

Theodore Roethke once wrote, "In a dark time the eye begins to see." As we have gradually become acquainted with the post-Holocaust, post-WWII world, we have learned some valuable lessons. One is that talking openly about issues is far preferable to ignoring them. Children are less anxious when their parents are honest with them about a given issue than when they ignore it or sweep it under a carpet. As Jonathan Kozol writes:

> The teacher who does not speak to grief, who cannot cry for shame, who does not laugh and will not weep, teaches many deep and memorable lessons about tears, laughter, grief and shame. When war is raging, and when millions of poor people are enduring both a private and communal Hell, no teacher, no matter what he does or does not do, ever fails to demonstrate a powerful bias in one fashion or another. This is the case even if his bias is conveyed only by the lesson of conspicuous abstention from a field already fraught with possibilities for moral indignation (1975: 138).

Young people know things are not well in this country; it makes them depressed and ultimately discouraged to see issues avoided. It seems that the problems *are* in fact insoluble if the adults cannot even acknowledge them. But talking about the issues, studying them, writing and doing projects about them empowers young people. Instead of being passive witnesses to decay, they become active participants in problem-solving. What we clearly do *not* need is another generation of political leaders willing to ignore posterity in favor of short-term acquisition and consumption. By then, there will be fewer resources for a new generation to acquire or consume. If we are to help the young become a positive force for the future, then we must have the courage to design curricula which are not just "relevant" (a word with negative 1960s connotations), but life-affirming and meaningful. We can, for example, still teach chronology and political events in history classes, but we can also take current problems and work backwards in time tracing how the present emerged from the past. In schools across the country, community service has become the basis of many academic programs. It is a proven way to combat apathy and alienation, and to *re*engage students in the whole enterprise of education. For example, we could ask each student in a given class to join a national organization such as Common Cause or Greenpeace or Save the Children Federation and to become familiar with that organization's goals, with the history of the problem(s) it is confronting, and with the legislation surrounding this problem. The students would learn about history, geography, economics, politics, social and environmental issues, but they would learn in a more hands-on context. Global studies programs, world cultures kits, multi-cultural educational activities packages now abound and can be found in curriculum centers, at textbook conferences and workshops, and at teacher institutes all across the country. In order to fully illustrate the growing gap between the rich and the poor, teachers may have to create units on their own, but there are several books immediately available from which to draw concepts, statistics, and illustrations. Such books would include:

Dee Brown, *Bury My Heart at Wounded Knee*
Jung Chang, *Wild Swans*
Linda Chavez, *Out of the Barrio*
Vine Deloria, Jr., *God Is Red*
Eduardo Galeano, *Walking Words*
Andrew Hacker, *Two Nations*
bell hooks, *Yearning: Race, Gender and Cultural Politics*
Paul Kennedy, *Preparing for the Twenty-First Century*
Oscar Lewis, *The Children of Sanchez*
Anne Phillips, *Democracy and Difference*
Ronald Takaki, *A Different Mirror*
Cornel West, *Race Matters*

In fact, assigning books such as these as required texts could be the basis of a senior high school history or social studies unit, a semester's work, or Advanced Placement or honors classes for the year.

We must not expect that twenty-first century leaders will just automatically appear; we must actively and consciously prepare young people for lives of active, caring social and political service. Now the word "politics" gives off rather a stench; it need not. Service should be considered as an honorable profession.

A Growing Disparity of Wealth

We saw in the previous chapter the startling statistics delineating the growing gap between the rich and poor on the world stage. It is no less true in America. One of our founding fathers, John Jay, rather accurately and baldly described democracy as he saw it and as it has remained: "The country should be governed by those who own it." In his day, it was the propertied classes. Black Americans were slaves with "3/5ths of a person status" in the Constitution, women didn't have the vote or ownership of land, children were exploited in gradually worsening conditions, and non property owners were virtually disenfranchised. Substitute the word "corporate" for "property" and John Jay's statement holds true today. The country is clearly divided along class lines even more strongly than racial lines; or, to put it another way, class issues subsume the racial issues: for example, rich blacks enjoy a far better life standard than poor whites. One should hasten to say that this is not the norm. The norm is that a small percentage of white males run the country—and not from Washington, D.C., but more from the corporate board rooms.

Now, saying this in schools and classrooms would be tantamount to belching at a D.A.R. tea or, at least, to running the risk of losing one's job. Saying it is so just isn't done. Yet why should this be? If the class structure is real and if the gap between the haves and have-nots is widening, then should it not be studied and analyzed? I recently attended a seventh grade class in a 99 percent black school where the teacher was teaching a civics lesson about the separation of powers in the three branches of government. It was a quaint lesson; yet utterly disconnected from the lives of these disenfranchised children. The real separation of power in this country is between class and race and this is what these children should have been studying—the history of class and race in America and what might be done to achieve greater equality of opportunity. It is ironic, sad, and even infuriating that so many poor and middle class Americans have bought the myths of democracy sold to them by the elite few who profit immensely by the apathy, passivity, and gullibility of that same many. As Noam Chomsky writes: "The people who are in control, who are harming others—those people will construct justifications for themselves" (1993: 73).

The 1980s were, according to many analysts, truly a heyday for the rich—a time comparable to the vast accumulations of wealth during the Gilded Age and the precrash Roaring Twenties. To call the 1980s—as has been done—a revolution is a rather bizarre use of the word, since it was the rich who were simply amassing even greater amounts of money while the masses fell further behind. Statistics bore most people, but a few startling ones illustrate the above rather well:

- The wealth share of the top 1 percent of Americans increased from 27 percent in the 1970s to 36 percent at the end of the 1980s.
- In the period 1984–88 the median net worth of U.S. households—assets minus debts—decreased by 4 percent.
- The tax cuts for the top 1 percent of Americans reduced their tax rate from 30.9 percent in 1977 to 23 percent in 1984—no other group gained nearly so much.
- During the period since 1977 the average after tax family income of the lowest 10 percent (in the $3,000 range) dropped by 10.5 percent. The incomes of the top 1 percent, which were only $174,498 in 1977, rose in a decade to $303,900—a whopping 74.2 percent increase.

As Kevin Phillips writes, "We are talking about a major transformation . . . no parallel upsurge of riches had been seen since the late nineteenth century, the era of the Vanderbilts, Morgans, and Rockefellers" (1991: 10). Surely changes of this magnitude warrant careful scrutiny. Surely they should be the subjects for study in social studies classes across the land. What, for example, we might ask, are the "American values" which allow our citizens and our governments to permit:

- an increasing number of children to fall into poverty and homelessness;
- our cities to fall into danger and disrepair;
- our schools to become overcrowded and filthy;
- ghettoes to evolve which are comparable to the worst slums in third world countries like Bangladesh?

Clearly these are questions that our next generation of citizens should consider rather than memorizing platitudes which describe a reality experienced by only the elite of the nation.

I have spoken of the disintegration of society and the breaking down of cities. Let us now consider each of these separately even though they are part and parcel of each other. In fact, each of the four topics of this chapter are interrelated. The breakdown of our cities and society amid the immense profiteering of the few at the expense of the many is a result of our spiritual drift. A society with a clear sense of priorities, decency, compassion, and justice would not allow what we allow, would not tolerate the intolerable. These issues must be acknowledged by educators and must be part of the substance of what we teach if there is ever to be any change.

The Disintegration of Community/Society

By disintegration I mean both the racial segregation that is growing in our cities, and the loss of a sense of societal unity and purpose. Throughout American history, certain social and political goals have enabled citizens to find a greater meaning in society than their own personal goals: creating a nation, acquiring new territories and establishing fifty states, rebuilding the nation after a civil war, building factories and developing industries, fighting two world wars—these were powerful galvanizing factors in creating a sense of national unity. But now there is a growing sense that we are floundering and confused. Churches are for millions no longer the center of their lives; simple farm communities have given way to absentee agribusinesses; cities seem sprawling metropolises without a center (as Gertrude Stein said of her childhood home in Oakland, "there is no there there"). In spite of heroic efforts by hundreds of civil rights advocates and idealistic community builders, we find racism a dominant force in America and desegregation projects in dire straits. The *Brown v. Board of Education* decision of 1954 might just as well have not happened judging by the segregation of school after school.

What can be done about this? Again, acknowledge its reality and use this topic as the basis for study in our schools. As we move toward a non–Euro-American majority, we need to broaden our definitions of culture, of American history, of what we mean by American values. America can no longer simply mean white. The Jefferson/Madison/John Winthrop vision of a homogeneous Anglo-American society is no longer a remote possibility even if it is a wish for a few. We must truly devise a whole new vision for America. *Time* magazine in 1990 reported that "by 2056, when someone born today will be 66 years old, the 'average' U.S. resident, as defined by census statistics, will trace his or her descent to Africa, Asia, the Hispanic world, the Pacific Islands, Arabia, almost anywhere but white Europe" (1990: 57).

For some whites, this is an unsettling turn of events. Certainly it is a dramatic demographic shift—one of the most dramatic in the history of humankind. It need not be violent or anxiety-ridden. It is an *opportunity* for *expansion*—two words and concepts which have been the hallmark of the American experiment. However, to take advantage of our new opportunities we must solve some basic economic problems. Ultimately, we cannot survive as a rich, white minority versus a poor multicolored majority. Violence and carnage will be inevitable. Schools are the place where we must lay the groundwork for a new society. As Ronald Takaki recently stated:

> I think schools are a crucial—probably the most crucial—site for inviting us to view ourselves in a different mirror. I think schools have the responsibility to teach Americans about who we are and who we have been. This is where it's important for schools to offer a more accurate, a more inclusive multicultural curriculum.
>
> The classroom is the place where students who come from different ethnic or cultural communities can learn not only about themselves but about one another in an informed, systematic and non-intimidating way. I think the schools offer us our best hope for working it out. I would be very reluctant to depend upon the news media or the entertainment media, which do not have a responsibility to educate. (Takaki, 1994: 15)

The Breaking Down of Cities

Recently I visited an inner-city elementary school and was shown around by the principal. About every third window was boarded up. "We cannot accept gifts of computers," she told me. "The gangs break in on the weekends and steal them." Another principal explained to me that he has his whole school trained to drop to the classroom floor or asphalt outside when they hear gunshots—an almost daily occurrence.

Children in American cities not only hear gunshots; they die from them. From 1979 to the present, about as many children have died in America of gunshots (over 50,000) as American soldiers died in Vietnam. Furthermore, we now have over

200,000,000 handguns in circulation on our streets and every two and a half years we kill the equivalent of our Vietnam dead on our own streets.

The list of other city ills is legion: gang wars, homelessness, "permanently unemployables," deteriorating streets, bridges, buildings, litter and graffiti and garbage everywhere, drive-by shootings, crime, drugs, unsolved murders and felonies, and on and on. None of these problems is insoluble. What we lack is not the means or even the knowledge of how to deal with each; what we lack is the will. Schools are the place to look at problems clearly and to inspire our young to attack them.

FDR and Churchill were able to inspire their countries to fight a war against fascism and imperialism. The evils in our own cities today are equally formidable and potentially as disastrous. This time, however, I do not believe we can look only to Washington for inspiration and leadership. Politics needs as much reform as our cities. No, this time, the inspiration must come from passionate educators, citizens, and parents who see what must be done and who motivate and encourage the young to find a sense of purpose in reinventing our nation.

Note

To prepare teaching units on demographic shifts, race, ethnic and class issues, immigration issues will require classroom teachers to go beyond standard textbooks. But again, there are numerous resources and organizations available to help teachers. For example, if a teacher wanted to offer a unit on Prejudice and Racial Intolerance, organizations like the Anti-Defamation League, the Intercultural Communications Institute, Teaching Tolerance, and others could be contacted at these addresses:

Anti-Defamation League
10495 Santa Monica Boulevard
Los Angeles, CA 90025-5031

The Intercultural Communications Institute
8835 SW Canyon Lane, Suite 238
Portland, OR 97225

Teaching Tolerance
400 Washington Avenue
Montgomery, AL 36104

Chapter 7

A New Cosmology:
Honoring the Blue Planet

This we know. The earth does not belong to man; man belongs to the earth. This we know. All things are connected like the blood which unites one family. All things are connected. Whatever befalls the earth befalls the sons of the earth. Man did not weave the web of life; he is merely a strand in it. Whatever he does to the web, he does to himself.

—Attributed to Chief Seattle, 1854

It's all a question of story. We are in trouble just now because we do not have a good story. We are in between stories.

—Thomas Berry, 1988

Name ourselves tree, grass, sun. Start over again from that point.

—Jimmy Santiago Baca

"My God—it's blue. It's beautiful." Perhaps the most startling photograph in the history of humankind was the photo of the earth from outer space. It was truly a revelation—the earth, all could see clearly, was—is—unique. It is an interconnected system of waterways, shining like a gem in the cosmos. Somehow, this photograph confirmed what only a supposed lunatic fringe had been arguing: that the earth is a precious jewel, utterly special, distinct, and interrelated. It is, we could now see, a tiny organism covered with a thin gorgeous blue membrane: water. The Blue Planet.

Physicists, astronomers, geologists, and others have now discovered and uncovered much of the story of how this blue planet came to be. It is a magnificent and mysterious story—the creation of the universe and the subsequent evolution of the earth with its systems of life. An amateur rendering of this story goes something like this:

> Somewhere between 8 and 20 billion years ago the universe sprang into being with what is now commonly agreed upon as The Big Bang, an instant "which set time, space, matter—everything—in play." This theory holds "that everything in the universe, including time, was once contained in a point of infinite density—a 'singularity'—that suddenly expanded [exploded] outward uniformly in all directions. At the age of one second, scientists calculate, the universe was a featureless fireball of uncertain size, a million times hotter than the surface of the sun and a thousand times denser than lead. At this point—of the Big Bang—there was only hydrogen for about seven seconds and then helium and carbon unfolded through the formation of galaxies, explosions of supernovas, and the universe continued to unfold with a growing capacity for greater and greater complexity. Then about five billion years ago, our sun, our solar system, and our planet came into being. And only just a blink ago human beings evolved. (Sawyer, 1995: 6–7)

When did all this occur? Scientists are still arguing, and with the arrival of new data from the Hubble telescope, new yet controversial estimates have ranged from as early as 8 billion years old to in the neighborhood of 12 billion—both downward revisions from previous and still respectable estimates of 15+ billion. Further, it is estimated that the particle known as the earth cooled and began its present orbit somewhere around 5 billion years ago. If, as Sister Miriam McGillis (*Fate of the Earth*, 1990) has charted, we compress that 5 billion years into a 12-month cycle, then we can see the following time-line unfolding.

During the first eight months, we find molten gases (still burning in the core of the earth), the evaporation of gases, and formation of the oceans and the earth's crust, the shaping of continents, and finally the appearance of amino acids and proteins and conditions which allowed life to form.

Four months ago (in our 5 billion years compressed into 12-month schema), the earth begins to show signs of life and we find the earth expressing itself in breathing, seeing, hearing; we find it learning to reproduce, nourish, and even heal itself; we find the earth becoming more and more complicated.

In the last four months, we see the development of highly complex creatures with central nervous systems.

THE HISTORY OF THE EARTH
4.6 Billion Years

Charted on a single year calendar. Each day represents 12 million years.
****

January 1—	12:01 to 12:03 a.m.—The origin of the earth (Big Bang)
February—	The first form of life—a simple bacterium
March—	
April—	Increasingly complex life forms
May—	
November 20—	The first fish
December 10—	Arrival of the dinosaurs
December 25—	Disappearance of the dinosaurs
December 31—	(afternoon)—The first prehuman ancestors
	11:45 p.m.—Homo Sapiens
	11:59 p.m.—All of recorded history.

Chart drawn from Robert Ornstein and Paul Ehrlich, *New World New Mind,* Simon and Schuster, 1989: 7.

If we take the last month and look at these 30 days, we see that the human being came upon the scene only in the last day. Then, if we look at only the last 24 hours, we see that 23½ hours were pre-ancient history, tribal days of the awakening of consciousness, the beginnings of language and social structures. The last 30 seconds is the period of the "great" civilizations. Thus modern history becomes just a few seconds. Yet, in these 2–3 seconds of the 5 billion year process, we humans have acquired the capacity to knock the whole process awry.

Thus, the human is not only a relative newcomer to the cosmos and to earth, but the human armed with technology and industry is a newborn—having possessed vast transformative skills for about 2–3 seconds in the scheme of things. And yet—as staggering a reality as it is—in those 2–3 seconds, humans have taken a 5 billion year evolutionary process and knocked it off its natural course. As McGillis puts it: "we have taken evolution off automatic pilot and put it on manual" (McGillis, 1990). We simply lack the maturity to do such a cataclysmic thing. We are destroying this blue planet. What has taken billions of years to evolve is being extinguished in this century in but a wink. Why?

Why we have taken our current course of destructive actions has many explanations. One, I believe, is the most comprehensive and—if we are to survive—must be studied by educators and transmitted to the young. This explanation comes largely from the works of Thomas Berry. Berry is a Catholic priest, cosmologist, ecologist, and former president of the Teilhard Society. He has published many papers from his now disbanded Riverdale Press, and he published his superb and major work, *The Dream of the Earth* in 1988 through the Sierra Club Press. He won a 1995 Lannan Award for his writing. For much of what has led to this point and which follows in this chapter, I am indebted to him and his work.

Every culture, every nation has its myths, its stories which give meaning to life itself and which provide the assumptions and values which in turn dictate how we live our lives. Most people, most teachers and students do not critically examine these myths and their underlying assumptions and guidelines. They are considered givens. The function of schools—all too often—is simply to inculcate these givens. Thus, from elementary school through to graduate school, certain basic myths are taught, ingrained, and celebrated in increasingly complicated presentations. The possibility that these very myths could be based upon faulty premises is rarely considered. So we are currently driving down a road leading to a precipice of annihilation and our education systems continue to talk about how well-paved the road is, all the while ignoring the precipice.

The Myth of Transcendence

Let us look at a few of these myths. First, we begin with our cosmology, our story of creation. The Judeo-Christian story deeply ingrained in the North American and European culture is that God created the earth, that God is transcendent to the earth, that heaven is up there, out there, somewhere over the rainbow, somewhere else. According to the myth, we humans are here for a brief time and then are transported elsewhere to our eternal afterlife. The earth becomes, in this myth, a temporary visiting place and we humans are for a time either its caretakers or its exploiters, but we are not coparticipants in the evolutionary process. Thomas Berry argues that humans are not just a stage in the evolution of the earth; we are *of* the earth. We are 70 percent water and 30 percent minerals just like the crust of the earth. We are star dust. We are the earth having cooled off and evolved over billions of years into homo sapiens. "Traced as far as possible in the direction of their origins, the last fibre of the human aggregate are lost to view and we are merged in our eyes with the very stuff of the universe . . . plurality, unity, energy: the three faces of matter" (Teilhard, quoted by Levitt in *Pablo Neruda Sky Stones*, 1990). Our uniqueness is our consciousness. We are the earth having become conscious of itself. Evolution did not end with the arrival of human beings; it continues in the growing consciousness of human beings. At present, we are gradually becoming conscious of our relationship to the earth. The earth is quite literally our mother and father. The earth is itself a living organism. If we injure it, we injure ourselves. If we destroy the earth, we destroy ourselves.

Berry observes that an outgrowth of the Judeo-Christian transcendence myth is "an intense preoccupation with the personality of the savior, with the interior spiritual life of the faithful, and with the salvific community," rather than with anything having to do with the natural world. "The essential thing is redemption out of the world through a personal savior relationship that transcends all such concerns." As humans have lost any mythic, visionary, or symbolic connections to the earth, the earth has come to be seen merely as matter to be used and exploited. "Because of this loss, we made our terrifying assault upon the earth with an irrationality that is stunning in enormity" (Berry, 1988: 126, 129, 135).

A second myth we have come to accept as a given is the myth of progress (see chapter 8). The myth dates back to the sixteenth and seventeenth centuries, which introduced the idea that we can improve life by harnessing nature through scientific discovery. The myth has sometimes even been expressed as man conquering nature. The scientific method led rather quickly to the industrial revolution and the technological age we now live in. As Berry points out, "Whatever their differences, both liberal capitalism and Marxian socialism committed themselves totally to this vision of industrial progress, which more than any other single cause has brought about the disintegration that is taking place throughout the entire planet. By a supreme irony, this closing down of the basic life systems of the earth (pollution of the water, soil, trees, and air) has resulted from a commitment to . . . progress" (Berry, 1988: xii).

In our schools, we must reexamine these two myths: the myth of transcendence and the myth of progress. The African-American activist, Stokely Carmichael, once said, "You are either part of the problem or part of the solution." The perpetuation of these two central myths *is* the problem, for both are leading humanity to self-destruction. If schools do not at least consider this possibility, then schools themselves are also part of the problem. It all goes back to an old argument—do schools exist to integrate the young into the existing culture or to foster genuine critical thinking and self-examination and cultural reevaluation? Most schools would argue they favor the latter, while unwittingly they support the former. It is crucial that we reexamine these myths and the role they play in encouraging our rape of the planet. For example, at the present time (1997) most educated citizens would argue that we have an ecological crisis. They might even agree that it was brought on by industry-technology, but they would probably then argue that our salvation lies in new and better technology and new and more industries. Somehow they believe that a heavier dose of the poison being used to kill the patient will save the patient. It seems misguided, but we are so immersed in the mythology we cannot see our way out. An old proverb states that you cannot solve a problem at the level of the problem. Yet this is exactly what we are attempting to do. This, of course, is assuming that we are trying to solve our ecological problems.

Reconsidering Economic and Environmental Concerns

Clearly, when any issue of saving the environment comes to the surface, a very real and complex issue also surfaces—jobs. When we seek to save forests, families who depend on the income from the lumber industry are, understandably, distraught and frightened. As more and more jobs disappear through technology, robotics, and "downsizing," then environmentalism seems but yet another threat to the economy. There are many ways to respond to this concern. Certainly the cost of saving the planet should *not* be to ruin the economic lives of families. Transitional guaranteed incomes along with job retraining until replacement jobs are secured is one way to assist families. No family should be rendered destitute by legislation to protect the environment. What is crucial, however, is that government leaders from the president of the United States to local representatives provide the citizenry with the enlightened leadership the times require. We cannot keep depleting finite resources forever. This is a truism. At some point, one generation of leaders and citizens must break the cycle of depletion, depletion, depletion. Parents must be educated to see that it is *not* good national parenting to destroy their children's heritage. Finally, jobs we mistakenly save today will make all of our tomorrows a blight. This is not only poor parenting; it is also lousy economics.

As Berry points out, "We are eliminating species at a rate never before known in historic time and in a manner never known in biologic time [that is at a rate unprecedented in 5 billion years]. Destruction of the tropical rain forests of the planet will involve destroying the habitat of perhaps *half* the living species of earth." The elitist few who are profiteering as a result of cataclysmic corporate power understand economics. They understand gross assets and net profit margins. They, however, miss a key point: "an exhausted planet is an exhausted economy" (Berry, 1988: 73-74). There is a deficit which will ultimately cause great harm to our children and our children's children and which contemporary profiteers do not factor into their balance sheets—it is the earth deficit. This deficit, the elimination of earth resources for human profit and utility, is a direct result of our view of the world—we do not see ourselves as part of a community of interrelated species utterly dependent upon each other—not only for survival but also for joyful witness and celebration.

Redefining Our Cosmology

Our cosmology, our understanding of the origins and structure of the universe is simply not adequate to meet the demands of our time. As Robinson Jeffers (1987: 195) writes: "Organic wholeness, the wholeness of life and things, the divine beauty of the universe. Love that, not man apart from that." Nevertheless, we have rapidly moved from economic development to ecological devastation. Somehow we need to marry the majesty and sophistication and mystery of the Big Bang story with the Native American understanding of our filial relationship to the land and its creatures. We need to traverse beyond nations and the United Nations to the United Species; we need to travel beyond capitalism and socialism to a planetary universalism; we need a new story and a new way of organizing and sharing the earth's resources. Capitalism/ Nationalism/Corporationism do not meet the needs of the planet. These needs of the planet are our needs. These are the issues our schools and teachers must at least discuss and bring to consciousness.

There is indeed a crisis. It must be met with awareness. We must all be educated to know what is being done to us and our 5-billion-year heritage. We must learn that species are being forever eliminated, trees decimated, lakes and seas polluted, and that our lives are being diminished by profiteers—all in the name of "progress." If schools neglect to teach these lessons, another generation of apathetic, passive citizens will become the profiteers who will further plunder the earth. Already the Blue Planet is changing its color. As I was writing this paragraph (September 1995), scientists and local residents were complaining that the beautiful blue Lake Tahoe in California is turning green. Blue skies we all know are turning gray and brown with layers of pollutants, and brown swaths of clear-cut forest graveyards are visible from satellite photographs. The Blue Planet is under deadly assault. Education is our first and most crucial line of defense.

EXAMINING SOCIAL ISSUES IN THE SCHOOLS

Chapter 8

Advancing to Less

The longer one lives in a reduced state,
the more reduced one becomes.

—Diane Ackerman

Not everything that can be done ought to be done.

—Herbert Zipper

Who is so rich that he can squander forever the wealth of earth and
water for the trivial needs of vanity or the compulsive demands of
greed; or so prosperous in land that he can sacrifice nature for un-
natural desires? The earth we abuse and the living things we kill will,
in the end, take their revenge; for in exploiting their presence we are
diminishing our future.

—Marya Mannes

At the conclusion of *Dirty Harry*, Clint Eastwood observes the
villain driving away in a car, thinking he has triumphed but
not knowing—as Eastwood does—that his car will explode in a
few seconds. After the explosion—which Eastwood has planted—
our hero laconically observes, "A man's gotta know his limitations." As a species we do not. In fact, we do not know that
limitation is a positive value. We have been so thoroughly im-
bued with the notion that progress is measured only by quan-
tifiable growth that we are failing to see several increasingly
obvious truths: that more is not always good; that the resources
of the planet are finite; that progress (as it is commonly now
defined) for the few at the expense of the many is unfair and
often criminal, not to mention ultimately destructive for *all*.

Until now, even voicing these concerns and questioning the
modern concept of progress has run the risk of branding the

questioner as un-American. But we all need to reexamine nine-teenth and twentieth century notions of progress and to place the idea of progress in the larger context of survival—a higher value. The Gospel of St. Mark 8:36 (St. James version) asks, "For what shall it profit a man, if he shall gain the whole world, and lose his own soul?" And to this question, we may add for what shall it profit a planet, if the few profit and we lose our own globe?

Myth of Material Progress

Few politicians will ever ask this question. Politicians get elected by assiduously avoiding such "long range" questions. They ask only, "How can I help my benefactors and constituents to make their own quick profits?" Posterity does not figure in politics. Consequently, educators must not only ask the questions; they must introduce a new generation of children to the idea that progress is not an end in itself. People are ends; material growth must benefit people or it is not progress. Killing all living elephants for the profit of the few today robs all human beings for all the tomorrows of the wonder and awe of admiring these creatures. The ivory trader's profit is not progress; it is merely greed and profligacy. As Edward Abbey writes:

> The religion of endless growth—like any religion based on blind faith rather than reason—is a kind of mania, a form of lunacy, indeed a disease and the one disease to which the growth mania bears an exact analogical resemblance is cancer. Growth for the sake of growth is the ideology of the cancer cell. Cancer has no purpose but growth; but it does have another result—the death of the host. (1988: 21)

Because political leaders of both parties will not draw—and too often cannot even see—this analogy, teachers and schools must lead young people to recognize the analogy. Unexamined progress is no longer (if it ever was) a value to be blindly worshipped. It is a by-product of a deeper ideology which itself must be reexamined: science/technology.

The scientific-industrial-technological revolution of the past 400 to 500 years has, within Western civilization, equaled, if not surpassed, the influence of religion in the lives of people all over the globe. Pure science, of course, is a strong and admirable expression of human curiosity, as is pure mathematics. But not every discovery needs to lead to a materialistic application. However, the current operating principle seems to be: "If it can be done, it should be done." And the benefits of science and technology—medicine, airplanes and automobiles, television and computers—are so widespread and seductive that even to examine the balance sheet of assets and liabilities of this revolution seems at best quixotic and at worst ignorant.

It is neither. This very balance sheet must be the stuff of every child's education. To proceed heedlessly chopping down rain forests; overdeveloping the land, polluting the air, water, and land, overproducing and, hence, expanding untreatable waste is progress for whom? Our fascination with technology has led us to destroy those very cultures to which we must now look if we are to survive. So called "primitive" cultures lived in harmony with the land. As Sister Miriam McGillis noted, the Native Americans lived on the land for a thousand years without changing it at all. European immigrants came and within 200 years had turned much of it into an urban blight. They did so in the name of the father—science; the son—technology; and the holy ghost—progress. When Francis Bacon first called upon mankind "to unite forces against the nature of things, to storm and occupy her castles and strongholds and extend the boards of human empire," Theodor Roszak notes that, "There was relatively little damage the human race could then do to its environment. The arrogance was as innocuous as it was exhilarating" (Roszak, 1973: 215). But now, we see the results of Bacon's New Philosophy and it is simply head-in-the-sand stupid to proceed "forward" as if we didn't know any better. We do know better. Yet our politicians are elected by the forces which profit from an ongoing rape of the planet. They are servants to the exploitative masters of the "profit-at-all-costs" ideology. Consequently, schools must take on the challenge of examining the values we have embraced which have led to the calamitous mess we are in.

Harrowing Questions for the Young

What must we do? Well, for one we cannot oversimplify. We cannot simply return to a preindustrial mode of economics and social organization. We have overpopulated the planet to such a degree that we are dependent upon technology and industry to feed, clothe, and house the globe. If that were not problem enough, we will be continuing our overpopulation of the planet in the coming half-century by a factor of anywhere from 25 to 50 percent. In addition, the mass communications revolution has only made more and more aspire to the very "blessings" which already threaten the very survival of all of us on the planet. Consequently, educators must at least pose a series of harrowing questions to our young people. The legacy of generations of profligate adults to children is now a series of seemingly insoluble problems. Yet, there is a spark of hope for us *if we* deal with the problems honestly and ask necessary questions. Some of these questions are:

- How can we distribute the resources of the planet in an equitable, just and environmentally sustainable manner?
- How can we find jobs and sustenance for people when entire industries must be dramatically curtailed, redirected, or even closed down altogether?
- How can we bridle economic profiteering and yet maintain an entrepreneurial democracy at home and even promote it abroad?
- How can we convince American entrepreneurs to help underdeveloped nations to become more self-sufficient and less dependent upon America?
- How can we find within ourselves as a nation the spirit of serving humanity even if it means that Americans would do with less?
- How can we convince people "that achieving an environmentally sustainable global economy is not possible without the fortunate limiting their consumption in order to leave room for the poor to increase theirs?" (Brown, Flavin, Post, 1991: 119).

These are but a few of the questions our schools must structure into their curricula. Growth is not one of the Ten Commandments. It is not even inevitable. As Abbey quotes Mark Twain: "Nothing is inevitable but death, taxes and the insolent dishonesty of elected officials" (Abbey, 1988: 23). Schools must confront our current dishonesty. For years we have all blithely accepted several wrongheaded notions. One is that there is some sort of "invisible hand" which directs, protects, and ultimately blesses the economy. Another is that we can measure progress by something called the GNP—the Gross National Product. A third notion is that technology somehow generates more new jobs than it displaces. All three notions have led us into a morass. The invisible hand is not only invisible; it is nonexistent. As one British economist writes: "New technologies almost always destroy more jobs than they create. . . . However, our unthinking reliance on the invisible hand has meant that we have failed to develop any mechanism to ensure that the overall gains from a new invention exceed the overall losses and that the winners compensate the losers. This is despite the fact that while a new process generally benefits those who introduce it, there is no guarantee that it will lead to gains for the community as a whole. As a result, economic growth can often mean a net loss of human welfare" (Douthwaite, 1992: 83–94). And, as long as we think that the *gross* (an apt word) national product is the only indicator of economic progress, we will continue to sacrifice human beings for the sake of an abstraction and the benefit of the few over the many.

Examining Resource Issues in the Classroom

Resource issues must be brought into classrooms across the land. Classroom teachers now have resources available to them from responsible environmental organizations all across the nation and the world. Teaching units, packets of materials for study, books and magazines abound. These materials also offer schools interested in designing integrated curricula with productive opportunities. For example, a social studies or U.S. history class might study a unit on trees in American history. They would begin with identifying indigenous trees, trees imported from other countries—when and why? Then they would examine what industries grow up utilizing trees, when the first forest services and protectionist agencies came into being, and why. Then they might study rates of depletion of trees as a resource. Meanwhile, math classes would use the statistics from these studies as a basis for mathematics problems and homework lessons. A science class might begin with Donald Culross Peattie's *A Natural History of Trees* and would study the natural functions of trees and perhaps conclude with Charles E. Little's recent, and terrifying, study, *The Dying of the Trees: The Pandemic in America's Forests*. Then the school might form clubs to write government officials—in the mode of Amnesty International—or add service to local tree-preservation groups to the community service opportunities for its students. Thus, the study would be reinforced by engagement.

Trees are but one example of how a curriculum can be organized around the study of a single issue. Soil erosion, the depletion of fish in seas and lakes, the disappearance of species—there are numerous opportunities not only to bring disciplines together, but to reexamine the myths which fuel our assault upon the environment. Once students see the rate at which forests are being eliminated, they may come to see more clearly that man's supposed transcendence of the earth and his need for growth are myths which are not only obsolete, but life-threatening.

Our schools and teachers need to encourage the next generation of consumers to look beyond purely materialistic measurements of "progress" and to consider other social indicators such as moral growth, the health and welfare and education of the many, and the sustainable development of the planet. "In 1972, the American Institute of Certified Public Accountants took up the cause and published a book exploring the issues, *Social Measurement*, which is no doubt still lying on many library shelves. The issues it explored are as relevant as ever" (Henderson, 1992: 59). It would be a demanding exercise for students—at all grade levels—to design their own list of social indicators of progress and to suggest ways we might try to measure a different kind of progress.

Finally, what does one say to those who believe that a guaranteed job sounds like communism or that asking Americans to do with less is a direct contradiction to the American dream of achievement and progress? To the former, I would argue that our ultimate goal must be to provide work for every American mentally and physically able to work. This utopian goal, however, must be tempered with the humanitarian value of caring for *all* people. Thus providing family payments for those put out of work by a changing economy and environmental preservation is not communism; it is decent nurturing of one's own community. As for the myth that "progress is our most important product," I can only say that over the centuries myths have often shifted to meet changing realities. We no longer sacrificially murder children to appease the gods. The earth is every human's heritage. The thin membrane of ozone which protects us all needs to be protected from exploitation which masquerades in the guise of progress. In short, we must review the whole myth of progress.

Of course, the central issue is a simple question. Wendell Berry asks it in the title of an essay of his: "What are people for?" As thousands of farmers lose their farms to bigger and fewer corporate (absentee-farmer) farms, no one stops to ask the question, "Is this good?" It leads to greater profits for the few. It is defined, by those who profit, as "progress." Berry writes:

> But these short-term advantages all imply long-term disadvantages, to both country and city. The departure of so many people has seriously weakened rural communities and economies all over the country. And that our farmland no longer has enough caretakers is implied by the fact that, as the farming people have departed from the land, the land itself has departed. Our soil erosion rates are now higher than they were in the time of the Dust Bowl.

> At the same time, the cities have had to receive a great influx of people unprepared for urban life and unable to cope with it. A friend of mine, a psychologist who has frequently worked with the juvenile courts in a large midwestern city, has told me that a major occupation of the police force there is to keep the "permanently unemployable" confined in their own part of town. Such a circumstance cannot be good for the future of democracy and freedom. One wonders what the authors of our Constitution would have thought of that category, "permanently unemployable." (Berry, 1990: 123)

Progress turns out to be a term which does *not* take into consideration quality of human life. It is simply a term expressing profit and/or loss. I grant that most people would dispute this notion; I also maintain that most would balk at even examining its foundations, its rationale. And that, I think, is a mistake, even a shame.

Somehow our society has drifted into acceptance of the notion that unlimited, unending economic growth is a natural law, a moral imperative, an economic necessity. It is none of these. Almost everyone in America has a generalized but clear sense that something is wrong. Economic growth since 1958 has been immense, yet few Americans believe that the quality of our life has improved. Quite the contrary, most feel it has declined. Yet no one seems to see that growth itself is a villain.

> On top of this failure to yield the satisfaction it promises, growth presents, of course an even more severe assault on our well-being. We are all familiar with the serious health threats associated with producing more and more: seepage of deadly chemicals into our water supply; toxic wastes that leach into our soil; acid rain that destroys life in our lakes and now seems to be affecting our own health; destruction of the ozone layer by fluorocarbons that greatly increases the risk of skin cancer and cataracts; pollution of the air by the exhausts of millions of automobiles and smokestacks; poisoning of our rivers by the waste products of industrial manufacture; dangers posed by nuclear power plants, both in disposing of their radioactive wastes and in the ever-present possibility of another Three Mile Island or Chernobyl—the list seems virtually endless. We all know about these dangers, and we probably all know that they are likely to shorten our lives and cause debilitating illness. Yet we have learned to live with them by employing psychological mechanisms of denial and avoidance. What we deny most of all is that it is the very essence of growth that these problems will increase exponentially, that what growth *means* is that we will continue to exploit the environment at a faster and faster rate. (Wachtel, 1988: 407)

Like the alcoholic who cannot deal with his pain and drinks even more, thus furthering his disease and ultimate demise, we are a nation addicted to the notion of growth, and though it is playing havoc with our lives and planet, we can only prescribe "more."

Schools must be the place where this is all reexamined. At each level of the curriculum, teachers need to fold into their studies questions about "why?" and "to whose advantage is this growth or change?" At my school, Crossroads, many science teachers see ethics as a legitimate and crucial aspect of their science classes. We do provide a required ethics class for twelfth graders, but ethical considerations should not simply be compartmentalized; they must be every teacher's concern. Thus a science teacher can also be a community service promoter. To illustrate, after teaching a unit on the pollution of the seas, the teacher might invite a spokesperson from a local organization. For example, in Santa Monica, we have made noticeable progress in reducing the toxicity of the Santa Monica Bay through the efforts of a group called Heal The Bay. Many of our science students have received community service credit working for this organization.

The Environmental Literature Canon

Also, given the dire environmental crisis which all humanity faces, I would argue that there is a canon of environmental literature every citizen, every student should read to be an educated person in the twentieth/twenty-first century. The "canon" will differ among various experts but I would certainly want every high school and college graduate to have read and understood several of the following:

Edward Abbey, *Desert Solitaire* (1968)
Thomas Berry, *The Dream of the Earth* (1988)
Wendell Berry, *The Unsettling of America* (1986)
Lester Brown, *The State of the World* (annual publication)
Helen Caldicott, *Toward a Compassionate Society* (1991)
Rachel Carson, *Silent Spring* (1963)
Mary E. Clark, *Ariadne's Thread* (1989)
Jacques Cousteau (film series on the oceans)
Dian Fossey, *Gorillas in the Mist* (1983)
Frances Moore Lappé, *Diet for a Small Planet* (1971)
J. E. Lovelock, *Gaia: A New Look at Life on Earth* (1979)
Helena Norberg-Hodge, *Ancient Futures: Learning from Ladakh* (1991)
Aurelio Peccei, *One Hundred Pages for the Future* (1981)
E. F. Schumacher, *Small Is Beautiful* (1975)
Henry David Thoreau, *Walden* (1854)

Honors classes, senior seminars, term papers and class projects in history/science/social studies/community-service classes all would use not only the above but an abundant source of books, articles, curricular kits and packages, computer programs—all easily available in bookstores, curriculum stores, and the like.

Ethics, community service, academic "solids," environmental classes and field trips—all are places to reexamine the myths and their consequences which threaten the land we walk on, the seas we sail, the soil from which we harvest food, and the very air we breathe. No class or series of classes is more important to study.

The next generation of leaders and consumers should be encouraged to consider a whole different set of priorities. Rather than profit and growth, the following priorities should at least be considered:

- Quality of life: leisure, number of hours of work versus vacation and family time.
- A guaranteed job for everyone.
- Preservation of wildlife, natural resources, and the environment.
- Elimination of gross poverty and inequities in society.
- Restoration of small, relatively self-sufficient farms and rural communities.
- Quality schools, hospitals, health plans and social services for all citizens.

Surely these are priorities most people would agree are laudable and valuable. Yet, we persist in following principles which lead in the absolute opposite direction. Why? Paul Wachtel quotes a story which partially explains our folly. The story tells of the drunk who is looking for his lost keys near a lamppost; when asked if that's where he lost them, he replies, 'No, I lost them down the block, but the light is better here.' Growth is the lamppost to which our politicians, both liberal and conservative, are drawn. But it is not where the solution to our society's problems lies (Wachtel, 1988: 411). Schools and educators must have the courage to move out from under the lamppost and to move into the shadows where we went astray and where we can seek to find our national soul and purpose.

Chapter 9

Who Will Tell the Children?

Wherever there is an interest and power to do wrong, wrong will generally be done, and not less readily by a powerful and interested party than by a powerful and interested prince.

—James Madison

They willingly traded everything they owned. . . . They were well-built, with good bodies and handsome features. . . . They do not bear arms, and do not know them, for I showed them a sword, they took it by the edge and cut themselves out of ignorance. . . . They would make fine servants. . . . With fifty men we could subjugate them all and make them do whatever we want.

—Christopher Columbus

The twin sibling myths of "man having dominion over the earth" and "growth/progress as our divine calling" are at the core of western and American civilization. With these myths, unquestioned and thoroughly absorbed into the culture, teachers and schools have provided generations of children their civics lessons. Across the land in history, social studies, civics, and government, and humanities classes, teachers explain to children how our democracy works—with checks and balances, local, state, and presidential elections, the Supreme Court, congressional debates, and so on. And the glazed, dewy-eyed youngsters memorize articles of the Constitution, the Bill of Rights, dates of elections and the like, and everyone has a nice warm, hot-chocolate kind of feeling. Now the children know how democracy works. Except for one problem: It doesn't and they don't.

Who will tell the children that democracy is not working in our country? Who will tell them that the few control our economy, purchase elections, make the rules, circumscribe the limits within which debate can occur, own the media and, therefore, select what news is fit to print? Who will tell the children that behind the charade of government theatrics are the corporate powers—both national and multinational—who call the shots and define how the game is to be played—including who shall win and who shall lose? Who will tell the children?

I believe that these questions must be addressed before we can expect any real change in our schools and our society. As long as the elitist powers determine that our schools shall remain underfunded, and as long as they perpetuate the nonsense that somehow this is inevitable and incurable, then facile and surface "reform" movements will be ineffective. There can be no genuine education reform without economic and political reform, and since the federal government and most state governments seem unwilling and/or unable to bring about such reform, shouldn't we ask several questions?

- Is the government capable of cleaning up the mess in our schools?
- Or is the government oblivious to how bad conditions really are?

Of course, both questions presuppose that the voting public would like better schools and, for the sake of argument, I am making that supposition.

I believe that the answer to the above questions is yes on both counts. But it would seem that congressmen and congresswomen, senators, and presidents are unwilling to make dramatic changes for fear of alienating the very financial backers who put them into office. Consequently, neither party is willing to make the kinds of changes which would make democracy really work and hence, which would lead to providing quality education for all children and not just the privileged few. So let us look at five reasons why democracy does *not* work, what would change this, and how this would lead to good schools.

One—Elections Are not Free,
Fair, or Representative

According to the textbooks our children are given, elected officials are supposed to represent "the people." They are not supposed to represent only the wealthy and corporate interests and their agendas. "However, it is unrealistic to expect our elected officials to operate in a system that requires each of them to raise millions of dollars in campaign contributions in order to get elected, and to raise those millions without any strings attached" (Lewis, 1996: 1). If both parties receive their funding primarily from corporations, it doesn't take a terribly astute person to see what the realities will be. Consequently, as campaigns have at all levels become increasingly expensive to run, we see that corporate funding and government favors have grown in tandem as the partners that they are. Antitrust litigation has all but evaporated, corporate taxes have been reduced, unions have been emasculated, and the interests and needs of "the people" and the children are of little consequence. Why should we expect it to be otherwise "when Republicans and Democrats alike get 70 percent of their campaign funds from corporate PACS in dolings serenely bipartisan" (Lewis, 1996: 26).

That buying of elections goes on is no surprise to anyone. Charles Lewis refers to elections as "auctions":

> The garishness of money in politics has reached new levels of audacity, and all within the law. For years critics of campaign finance, such as the late Philip Stern, have described our legislators as "the best Congress money can buy." But these are truly glorious days in Washington for industry lobbyists and lawyers, who represent everyone from corporations that pollute and tobacco companies to the largest banks, real estate, and insurance companies. These corporate interests have raised and contributed vast sums of money—tens of millions of dollars—to those in power. Their representatives now sit in Capital Hill hearing rooms side by side with the members of Congress they helped to elect, together drafting new laws on such issues as clean air, clean water, workplace safety, information technology, and public health that will affect every American. There is no longer even the polite pretense of an open, honest debate between opposing interests. Amidst Washington's mercenary culture, in which wealthy private interests play an increasingly crucial role, the impression is unmistak-

able and indelible that our government—theoretically of the people, by the people, and for the people—is actually being sold to the highest bidder (Lewis, 1996: 11).

What is surprising is how little public outrage there is to combat it. Here there are various theories—people are too cynical to think it could ever be different; those who could change the system are its current beneficiaries; apathy and despair are rampant; the media carefully avoids whipping up any public outrage—since the media knows where its bread is corporately buttered; and since the legislators who could legislate campaign reform were themselves elected by the current rotten system— why change it? The truth is probably all of the above. So, what can we do about it?

For openers, we could tell the children (the next generation of voters) the simple truth. Tell them that our democracy is not working and that it is up to their generation to provide the leadership and energy so sadly lacking in the current government and citizenry. We could also tell the children how this current situation came to be and how we have allowed it to happen. We could also suggest changes that might be beneficial: for example, the idea that political contributions from the private sector (including one's own money) must be prohibited in campaigns for public office, that a one-cent sales tax or a one-dollar income tax fee be used to fund all elections, that all candidates for any office be allotted *equal* time on television and radio (speeches and debates should be allowed but advertising should be prohibited—a candidate is not a bar of soap), that voting be mandatory—all as they are in Australia. Ideas must be aired and discussed before they can ever become law, but since our "elected" officials rarely discuss these ideas, then why not discuss them in school? Instead of perpetuating fairy tales about free elections, why not tell the children that elections are often bought, that this is wrong and needs to be changed. This leads to a second reason why our democracy is not working.

Two—The Phony Debate

In addition to the myth of free elections, schools also unwittingly perpetuate the additional myth of the two-party system.

In reality, there is one political party in America—the "Republicrat" or "Demopublican" party, and Americans go to the polls every four years (to vote for president) thinking they are making meaningful choices. But the choices are all to the right of center. Currently, both parties are trying to lure voters with taxcuts but neither party is suggesting tax increases to clean up our cities, build new schools, or repair the infrastructure of the country. Both parties are critical of welfare abuses, but neither party is willing even to consider that the present economic system is tantamount to a corporate welfare state and to suggest ways of redistributing the disparate wealth which the rich are amassing as the poor get poorer. As Gary Wills writes, "There is no political left in America, though the Republican party still beats that nonexistent dead horse" (1991: 13). So for those who believe reform is critical to the health and well-being of the United States it matters little whether a Republican or Democrat is elected to office—neither party is willing to address reform. Why? Again, because both owe their very existence to the current system. They are the paid servants of the oligarchs who are prospering so immensely from the way things are. How can this be, one might ask? This leads to reason three (although we begin to see the reasons are interconnected).

Three—The Media Smokescreen

The third reason why the one-party system flourishes is that the media—which are owned by the owners of the "two parts" of the one party—the media create the illusion of a real debate between the "two parties" for those few interested in "debate." For the rest of the population the media serve to entertain and distract from any *real* issues. Thus, the media have two major political functions: One, to perpetuate the myth of democracy-in-action and two, as Noam Chomsky writes, to keep the "bewildered herd bewildered" (1992: 95). To achieve the first goal, the press designs, implements, and distributes "debates" in which a great deal of heat is often generated. Republicans call Democrats leftists, liberals (a new sneer word), pinkos, socialists, radicals, etc. . . . While Democrats call Republicans right wingers, extremists, fascists and the like. It looks like a real, wild debate is going on. People get agitated; they yell and call names and the American public is led to believe that significant differences exist between these two antagonists. Meanwhile, the oligarchs—who fund both parties—enjoy the spectacle because reforms which might diminish their disproportionate wealth are never discussed. The media know that is their job to protect the wealthy by not letting the public know that they exist.

> The American oligarchy spares no pains in promoting the belief that it does not exist, but the success of its disappearing act depends on equally strenuous efforts on the part of an American public anxious to believe in egalitarian fictions and unwilling to see what is hidden in plain sight (Lind, 1995: 36).

Part of the reason why the public is unwilling to see what is hidden in plain sight is that the mythology of a two-party system represented by *freely* elected officials is imprinted on children in schools and because the media then bow down before their masters and seemingly verify the mythology. As Gore Vidal writes, "another of our agreed upon fantasies is that we do not have a class system in the United States. The few who control the many through opinion have simply made themselves invisible" (Vidal, 1992: 56). Thus, the first place to break free from this brainwash is to educate the next generation of voters as to just what hogwash this brainwash really is. Schools could, at least, discuss the possibility that there are reasons why the gap is widening between rich and poor in America and why the government *seems* oblivious to this fact.

Four—The Government Lies

There is a fourth reason why our supposed democracy is not working. It is a difficult subject to expect schools to treat. Yet the evidence is overwhelming. Government *seems* to be many things. But government and its elected officials often lie—not always, but often enough. And when caught, they will simply say, "I mis-spoke." Thomas Jefferson wrote, "if a nation expects to be ignorant and free, it expects what has never been nor never will be." Yet how can a citizen be anything but ignorant when he or she is not told the truth? No one in government has been willing to fully discuss with the American people the extent of government responsibility for the savings and loan crisis. Recently, former Secretary of Defense Robert McNamara wrote a book telling the American people that he, in effect, lied on TV to the nation about the course of the Vietnam war. The examples, and books, are legion. Again, rather than simply spooning propaganda to our young, why not study examples of government deceit and discuss what political consequences and citizen resources are available? Why not discuss in school the ethical issues we want our children to care about? Where else are they going to learn of these issues? Certainly not from the media. History classes need not avoid examples of government deceit in an effort to inculcate a sense of national pride in the young. Indeed, as E.M. Forster wrote in giving "two cheers for democracy," it is one of democracy's glories that it can criticize itself (1938).

Perhaps the best way to prepare the young for future citizenship is to alert them to the dangers of gullibility and to the necessity of truly free and open debate. A great deal can be learned about democracy by studying examples of government deceit. So, I would want included in any American history class— at any grade level—an examination of recent events where we now know that the government did not tell the truth to the American people: the Tonkin Gulf incident, Watergate, the Iran-Contra affair, the bombing of Cambodia, the Panama-Noriega debacle, the savings and loan crisis, the CIA/Allende/ Chile actions, and the covert actions against Nicaragua. Students are not demoralized by reading about and discussing such events. On the contrary, they are empowered when they are presented with attempts to discover the truth. Learning after a given class that they were spoon-fed pablum is truly demoralizing and produces cynicism. If we are to avoid producing a new generation of demoralized, disengaged, and cynical citizens—surely the death knell of a democracy—we might try a novel approach to the teaching of politics—seek the truth wherever it leads.

Five—The Corporate State v. Popular Sovereignty

Michael Parenti has defined the U.S. polity as a dual system. On the one hand, there is the system we are taught in schools, what the media spoons out, the elections, the whole popular and public system. Then there is the hidden system referred to above, the oligarchy, what Parenti refers to as the "State." The State, he writes, "has little, if anything, to do with popular rule or the creation of public policy. It is the ultimate coercive instrument of class power (Parenti, 1995: 6). How this translates into action is that the elites, the oligarchies, the capitalist-corporate rulers of America utilize government policies and control elected officials to preserve their status of wealth and invisible power. They denounce government, all the while taking advantage of government grants, loan guarantees, tax credits, land giveaways, price supports, tax loopholes and reductions, and various other government subsidies. The very existence of corporations as "persons" in the Constitution is one of the more blatant forms of the sanctioning of corporate welfare. It is so rooted in our national assumptions that no one ever stops to examine its implications. So, as Parenti observes, when the powerful say they want less government, "they are referring to human services, environmental regulations, consumer protection, and occupational safety, the kinds of things that might cut into business profits" (1995: 7).

While this is so, schools across the country teach civics and political science and history as if our democracy were functioning merely as a popular sovereignty, as if there were no such thing as a corporate state. It is not so much that no one sees that the emperor has no clothes; it is more that no one acknowledges that the emperor even exists. Until the citizenry gains this awareness, there can be no meaningful change or creation of a true democracy. This awareness must come from the schools.

In summary, we need to teach our next generation of students/voters how to make democracy work for all the people and not just the elite. We need to examine in schools at all ages how things presently work and what might be done to rectify them. At present, less than 50 percent of registered voters vote in any election (18 percent elected the Republican congress in 1994), only wealthy or wealth-backed politicians can run for office, political debates in the media are all to the right of center, the truly wealthy and powerful remain invisible, the class structure of America is ignored, government officials frequently lie, and government supports the corporate state rather than "the people."

All of this adds up to a dysfunctional system. Rebuilding the system only can occur after we acknowledge, study, and fully understand the dysfunctional elements. Schools are traditionally places of deep encrustation and reactionaryism. Why? Because teachers tend to teach what they were taught. Consequently, the whole system conspires against change. The Constitution favors the propertied class, the politicians serve it, the media propagandize and mindlessly protect it, and the schools teach that it all works beautifully. So what is the problem, one might ask?

Postscript: I asked a leading New York editor to read this chapter and his response was as follows:

> This particular topic seems most likely of all to ignite a firestorm of resistance and debate in the community, since the required civics and government courses seem to function almost as a quasi-religious catechism of American identity. I can hear squawks from some if these were tampered with, though the time may be propitious in some ways, since even conservatives are saying that the system doesn't work, and there's increasing interest in a third party. History classes are already a focus of debate—I've seen stories in textbooks that feature blacks, women, and Native Americans, but don't mention Paul Revere. In this context, your proposals look like matches tossed in spilled gasoline. Fine, but a little more detailed battle plan might be helpful. Your last paragraph [just before the postscript] in this chapter acknowledges the inherent resistance within society and schools themselves to open discussion on these matters, but ends only with irony. What are some ways to overcome this resistance—how could a principal work on this, or an individual teacher? (Withers, 1996)

I confess the questions threw me for a loss at first. I had thought this chapter—Who Will Tell the Children?—was clear. Teachers would ask the hard questions in class and students would learn by confronting these hard questions. But if the editor is correct,and principals and teachers will ferociously resist the questioning of any "quasi-religious catechism(s) of American identity," then what can I suggest? Seemingly, we have a Catch-22 situation: the next generation of children whom I would like to see bring about change is being taught by those opposed to change. What indeed would be some ways to overcome this resistance?

A Plan for Action

Well, I would begin by repeating that democracy in America is malfunctioning for both liberals and conservatives alike. The loss of jobs, downsizing, the decline in value of salaries for the middle class, the growth in violence and crimes against citizens at large affects liberals and conservatives equally. It is not un-American to try to improve the quality of life for our children; in fact, constructively criticizing our own government is as American as apple pie. But saying this is so is not an action plan. So here is a modest sort of an action plan.

One, we should expand the range of institutes, workshops, and conferences for principals and teachers to study the state of American democracy. Organizations like Common Cause, The National Commission for Economic Conversion and Disarmament, the A.C.L.U., the NAACP, Statewide Organizations for Tax and Campaign Reform, The Sierra Club and The Yosemite Institute, and so on, must become more aware of the need to teach teachers and not just seek to enlist the support of an older generation which is already immured in the old myths. Change will most likely come from a younger generation, but only if *their* teachers at least help them to formulate new questions. Across the country workshops do ask tough questions, but there are too few of them and too often they preach to the choir. Somehow the leaders of these workshops need to find ways to attract the unconverted. I have found, for example, that offering stipends to attend such conference/workshops will lure underpaid teachers to seek further education. In addition, we need to find funding sources for institutes willing to actually study the relationship between American myths and the malfunctioning of democracy.

Second, (and this is already beginning to happen), we need to create new schools which have enlightened reform built into the curriculum from the start. Many of these schools will need to be independent (private) schools since their very essence is to encourage independence of mind and action among their graduates. For example, the New Visions Foundation in Santa Monica, California, is dedicated to designing and creating new schools whose goal is not only academic excellence but also an integrated and involved community. Its first venture, New Roads School, opened in September of 1995, serving grades 6, 7, and 8. The Foundation believes that Los Angeles is facing twin evils: segregation and ghettoization, and the New Roads School curriculum attempts to combat both. In its history classes, the traditional stories, i.e., Paul Revere, are taught, but so is Howard Zinn's *People's History of America*. Traditional civics lessons are embodied in the curriculum, but so too are the questions and issues raised earlier in this chapter. Across America, new schools are emerging which take a more grass roots approach to the study of democracy. These schools are funded by private investment by supporters—some conservative, some liberal (the New Visions Foundation board is a blend of both)—who believe that the restoration of participatory democracy can only strengthen American.

Third, I believe we need to fund for principals more ongoing forums which encourage broader vision and more bold action. To illustrate how both can come about, eight years ago a fellow educator, Jack Zimmerman, and I organized a monthly roundtable of private-school headmasters to meet and discuss our issues, to question each other's fundamental assumptions, to try to get beyond the normal institutional posturing which so often accompanies administrative confabs and to deal with issues crucial to children and society. It has worked. In fact, looking back, we are all rather amazed at how honest and mutually supportive we have become. As a consequence of this support, each of us has become somewhat bolder in effectuating change at our respective schools. We have borrowed ideas, shared programs and assemblies, and organized retreats together. We have also established such a level of personal trust that we can share confidences, problems, and fears at a level which I believe is quite unusual.

Because this has worked so well with our New Visions group, Jack Zimmerman and I decided to go one step further and establish a New Visions II group of private *and* public school principals and administrators, and that group has now been meeting, in council fashion (see chapter 4) and has reached, very quickly, the same level of trust as Group I. The issues we have dealt with in Group II have included racism and classism in the school, faculty apathy and anti-adventurousness, parental absence in the school communities, administrative stultification and timidity, and a host of tough questions. Both groups have the same facilitator, Jack Zimmerman, and having an outside facilitator enables each of us to come to the table prepared to be a participant only and to be challenged. The group has also led to action: one public school principal has become far more involved in fundraising for new programs, another has instituted a brand new human development program in her middle school, a third has organized her parents to fight, successfully, a bureaucratic plan to relocate her just after she was making progress (this would have meant five principals in seven years for her school). The group gave her the courage to rise up and say "no" to the mindlessness of the system.

Have Groups I and II dealt with the issues of American myths and the dysfunctions of democracy? Only tangentially, but the venue for discussion is in place and we will soon, at my request, be covering these topics. In fact, this chapter will be the focus of a forthcoming meeting.

Are these suggestions adequate answers to my editor's question: How could a principal work on this, or an individual teacher? I am not certain. Perhaps they offer a start.

Chapter 10

Crossroads: A Carnival That Works

Two roads diverged in a yellow wood and I
I took the one less traveled by,
And that has made all the difference.
                    —Robert Frost, "The Road Not Taken"

My name is Teresita Del Carmen Marroquin—but Terry's fine. I was
born in Los Angeles and raised, in many ways, on its streets. Because
of Crossroads School, I stand before you as the first in my family to
attend college, and I have a new and different life from the one I
would have had.
                    —Terry Marroquin, Graduation, June 1996

Nestled between a freeway and a major boulevard, between
20th and 21st Streets in Santa Monica, California, Crossroads
School occupies fourteen remodeled industrial and commercial buildings—some owned, some leased—with an alley running down the middle of the campus. A *Los Angeles Times* re-
porter once wryly referred to the school as having "all the
ambiance of a tire factory." At any given time, promenading
up and down the alley is a diverse and talented student body,
saying hello to their teachers on a first-name basis, and, by
their very carriage and demeanor, making it clear to even the
most casual of observers that these are students who enjoy
their school. Visitor after visitor, for over two decades now,
will observe, "You know, these kids seem to really like school."
It is a goal of the school: to have students look forward to coming to school each day. Our startling theory is that happy people
tend to be more productive and do better work than unhappy
people.

In 1984, Crossroads School was selected by the U.S. Dept. of Education as one of sixty exemplary private schools in America. Prior to receiving the award, the school was visited by two representatives of the exemplary schools selection committee (two former school principals) who told me, as headmaster at the time, that they had "never seen such a carnival that worked so well." I was delighted, for the word "carnival" captured much of what I had wanted the school to become when a group of us founded it fourteen years before: joy, diversity, warmth, intellectual vitality, a sense of aliveness and creativity, a festival of unique individuals. At its best, the school combines a demanding academic program with a kind of relaxed zaniness which enables everyone to laugh, to learn, and to enjoy the moment, and not see the moment as just preparation for future moments. Teachers are inspired by a learning environment that is self-sustaining and self-expanding: that is, in an atmosphere of open inquiry where students are urged to ask questions, to challenge convention, so that the teachers are inspired to grow as well. It is a feedback system with give and take in which both teacher and student are invigorated. How the school came into being, what makes it unique, and where it is planning to go may be of some relevance to the overall themes of this book. At least, I hope so.

The Birth of a New School

There was more than the usual discontent with public schools in 1970–71: A teachers' strike was rumored, the press was writing rather harsh articles about public education, and all this coincided with a series of events in my life—all of which made the launching of Crossroads School a serendipity. In June of 1970, I had accepted an offer to become the headmaster of a private, church-related elementary school—St. Augustine's By-the-Sea Episcopal School. The school was an old-fashioned, rigid, and, I concluded, rather sterile place. Children were treated like miniature adults (they marched from classroom to classroom in a column of twos with their hands folded behind their backs). There were virtually no arts classes; there was no racial or ethnic diversity, and no innovative approaches to learning. Within the first week, primarily out of naiveté, we changed the school 180 degrees. We added the arts, eliminated letter grades, opened up the classrooms, instituted group and cooperative learning centers and projects, offered elective classes, admitted a racially, ethnically, culturally, economically diverse student population. Very quickly the debris hit the fan. Parents withdrew their children, new families entered, and within two years, we had a 100 percent turnover in faculty and about a 70 percent turnover in families. I do not recommend this approach, but strangely, and in retrospect, it was fortunate, for in a short period of time, a consistent new philosophy had been implemented and the school became—and still is—an exemplary place.

During that first September of 1970, when the transformation was in its rather chaotic early stages, a group of sixth-grade parents—happy with the changes—came to me and said, "Where do we go next year?" I blithely replied, "Let's start a school." You see, I had been daydreaming of starting a school since my undergraduate years and had met a new friend in 1969, Dr. Rhoda Makoff, who also wanted to start a new school. In fact, when I became headmaster in June of 1970, she had joined me as my assistant. So, we seized the opportunity and suggested to these parents that we start a new school the following September. They were excited and, to make a long story short, in September we opened a seventh and eighth grade with thirty-two students. A simple chart will illustrate our subsequent growth:

	1970–71	1996–97
Enrollment	32	1009
Grades	7–8	K–12
Campus	2 rented classrooms	14 buildings (½ owned; ½ leased)
Faculty: Full	2	88
Part	10	54
Total Budget	$45,000	$15 million
Financial Aid	$4,500	$1.7 million
Capital Fund Raising	0	$5.8 million
Annual Giving	$2,000	$940,000

Of course, the real story is not growth per se. The exciting story is what has emerged. And what has emerged, I believe, is a function of a philosophy of education to which we have tried at all times to be true. The school philosophy has been virtually unchanged in twenty-five years. Other schools have come into being and died out (the same year Crossroads was created, seven other schools were born in our same part of town; only two remain). The philosophy was wise and child-centered, and has been the yardstick by which we measure ourselves and our programs. It has provided us with a consistent identity. It is as follows:

> Crossroads School was founded upon five basic commitments: to academic excellence; to the arts; to the greater community; to the development of a student population of social, economic, and racial diversity; and to the development of each student's physical well-being and full human potential.
>
> It is the goal of Crossroads School to provide a strong college preparatory program from which each student will develop a personal commitment to learning, a respect for independent thinking, and an expanding curiosity about the world and its people. We consider certain skills to be essential for all graduates: to read well, to write clearly and coherently, to study effectively, to reason soundly, and to question thoughtfully.
>
> Through the academic process we assist students to gain self-worth, self-knowledge, and respect for the knowledge and opinions of others. We believe that education must not be a race for the accumulation of facts, but should be an enriching end in itself. We also believe that education is a joint venture among students, parents, and teachers. To be effective with young people, teachers and parents must themselves continue to learn so that they may perceive the young accurately and treat them wisely.
>
> We believe that the arts are an essential part of the curriculum and that it is important for students to express themselves creatively and to use their imaginations freely. Therefore, music, drama, visual arts, film, writing, and dance are significant parts of student life at Crossroads.
>
> Through our academic and extracurricular programs we seek to promote social, political, and moral understanding and to instill a respect for the humanity and ecology of the earth.
>
> We understand that there are many kinds of intelligence and the traditional academic, cognitive area is one. Other important areas of intelligence are intuition, imagination, artistic creativity, physical expression and performance, sensitivity to others, and self-understanding. To neglect any of these areas is to limit students in the development of their full human potential.
>
> We believe the uniqueness of children is revealed in their very existence and that it is the school's responsibility to foster their innate sense of the mystery and joy of life.

What we have learned is that this philosophy works. It reminds us that children and young people are not merely academic functionaries, but are complex, emotional beings whose inner lives are mysterious and fragile, and that it is our responsibility as educators to nurture and respect that inner world. When we do, students respond in ways that would melt the hardest of hearts. When we treat school as a joyful carnival, they eagerly look forward to coming to school each day. Over and over our parents tell us their children are sad when summer vacation comes. Initially, some people were suspicious of whether real learning could occur in such a happy place; yet gradually they became convinced, and now, after almost twenty years of graduating senior classes, even the most skeptical have become believers. Each year, 100 percent of the graduates successfully attend colleges such as Yale, Stanford, Harvard, and Berkeley. I believe that it is the attention to the inner world of children and young people which enables them to succeed in the outer world of classes, tests, term papers, and later, jobs, families, and human relations. Most people do not flunk out of life academically or intellectually; they flunk out emotionally. They do not have a vocabulary or set of conceptual frameworks to deal with the whole range of human emotions. To this end, we have instituted weekly council and mysteries classes for every student, and a comprehensive human development department. We believe that learning about one's inner self and one's self-in-relation-to-others is certainly as important as algebra or English grammar. The complexities and confusions of modern life demand attention, and attention paid will return positive dividends.

The Joy of School

Perhaps the most joyful results of implementing our philosophy has been joy itself. Treat young people with respect—that is, honor individual uniqueness, encourage its self-expression, acknowledge with kindness and gentleness its confusions and fears, respect its privacy—and they will respond in creative and productive ways. Most important, they will bring an infectious sense of happiness to their studies and activities. School becomes a place where the human spirit flourishes.

One thing we have learned in launching and nurturing our carnival is that we must provide our students with as diverse a curriculum as possible so that each student may find his or her passion—be it the arts or community service, or Latin, or science. For once a student finds an activity that kindles his/her passion, that passion will spread into other subjects; lessons learned here will be transferred to there; life suddenly takes on meaning and there is a reason to want to go to school each day. Of course, one must find dynamic teachers whose enthusiasm is contagious. Such teachers come to class on fire; they feel they *must* convey to their students how important this theorem is, that treaty, this scene, that experiment. Students see in their day-to-day existences far too many people who are disengaged from what they do in their lives and work. When these students see the real thing, they want it.

The Basic Curriculum

How does this diversity of curricula manifest itself? On the surface, there are the usual "five solids" which every student is required to take: history, English, math, science, and foreign language, and within each are the various traditional classes. In addition, there are the academic electives—i.e., film (history, criticism, aesthetics), anthropology and ethics, creative writing; often these change from year to year, as teachers wish to teach new courses. Last, there are the other graduation requirements: the arts, community service, and human development. Within each of these are relatively large departments and classes.

Consider the music curriculum, which has grown from a single music history class and a ragtag jugband in 1970 to one of America's leading high school music programs. Now the school has developed a chamber ensemble (twelve violins, four violas, four celli) which is one of the finest in the world. It has featured guest soloists such as Yo Yo Ma, Emanuel Ax, and André Previn, all of whom were astonished by the orchestra's quality. These students not only have four hours a week of rehearsal, but they take six hours a week of music theory—which includes harmony, counterpoint, ear-training, composition, and music history. Also, they have a chamber music program with guest coaches and solo recitals. Routinely, they test out of the first two or three years of college theory—even at leading conservatories. But it is not just the challenge of the curriculum which makes the student's experience special. It is the daily contact with peers who are dedicated and talented, with teachers who are in love with their teaching, with a slightly zany school atmosphere and with its diverse curricula, which enables these students to go beyond being grinds or "music nerds" and instead to become more complete human beings. In addition to these "music majors," the school provides two jazz bands, three choral groups—including an advanced group (The 21st Street Singers) who have now developed a statewide reputation. The school has embraced the notion of seeking genuine excellence in several areas—one of which is certainly music.

Or consider the community service program, which consists of two full-time equivalent teachers and a rich menu of community opportunities to satisfy each student's graduation requirement—opportunities ranging from working at Head Start centers, to soup kitchens, to senior citizens homes. There are dozens of placement opportunities. Consequently, large numbers of our graduates have ultimately selected service occupations and have said their Crossroads community service placement gave focus and direction to their selection of a college major and a career.

Or consider our human development-mysteries-council program. This thirteen-year-old program (K–12) gives students ways of understanding and dealing with relationships, with stress, with separation and loneliness (and sometimes death), with family, with the whole range of adolescent confusions and developmental issues. I cannot imagine trying to educate young people without dealing with all these issues; yet all across the land schools do try—and all too often they fail. The mysteries classes (called "life skills" at grades six to eight, "connections" at grade nine, and "mysteries" at grades ten to twelve) provide a safe, confidential place for this to occur. The students are genuinely grateful for these classes. Many, upon graduation from a Princeton or a Northwestern or an M.I.T., will tell us their mysteries class was the most important class in their entire education. Seniors are particularly appreciative of their four-day retreat, which is the culmination of their mysteries class and which itself culminates in a genuine Native American sweat lodge ceremony—carefully prepared for as a rite-of-passage. This "sweat" and a preparatory "vision quest" period of "alone" time has a profound impact on these seniors. They return to Los Angeles (from a retreat center in Ojai, California) transformed. Their parents often note a new maturity, sensitivity, and greater awareness of the importance of family, friends, and school. Many will return to Ojai on their own in later months and years to do a follow-up vision quest.

The separation of church and state in our education systems has led to a great spiritual vacuum for many students. There is an absence of ceremony, of a sense that there is anything which transcends "me." We give students no place to talk of the spiritual dimension of life. In fact, we prohibit it. Certainly, I am *not* arguing for the inclusion of sectarian studies in schools. But I do believe that Crossroads has evolved a process that works for young people. The simple acknowledgment of life's mysteries and the ceremonial honoring of people's feelings and interior lives helps young people to feel that there are avenues available to them to explore their interior world without being overwhelmed or controlled, and that there are ways of dealing with relationships that are safe and often productive. It is a great gift we give our students and certainly to ourselves as teachers and administrators. For it is impossible to sit in council with young people without learning yourself, and without being challenged to grow.

When I look back over the past twenty-five years of Crossroads' birth and development, I am perhaps most proud of the risks we have taken with individual students. We have, for example, admitted many disadvantaged minority students and, after years of tutoring, counseling, affection and nurturing, we have sent these students on to four-year colleges where they have succeeded and emerged into society transformed, self-aware, and productive. When R. came to Crossroads in the tenth grade, he was reading at about a fifth-grade level. He was, in effect, a street kid whose parents' whereabouts were unknown. He was homeless and rootless. He had one sibling, a brother, who begged us to take him, and we did. The faculty was at first dismayed. How could he survive in our academically demanding school? But they rolled up their sleeves and went to work—tutoring, encouraging, spending weekends and weeknights helping him. One of our school families took him into their home—now ten years later he still lives with this family while working part-time and going to college. His life has been turned around.

R. was an extreme case but not atypical of risks we have taken. The school budget now alots 1.7 million dollars to financial aid—out of a 15-million-dollar operating budget. This is 12 percent off the top; each dollar awarded in aid is tuition income the school could receive (from waiting lists) but forgoes. Each year, we admit students who need to catch up from the ill effects of previous lack of schooling, parenting, and neighborhood disfunctioning. Crossroads provides both education and order for students emerging from what one writer refers to as the "crazy chaos" of the ghetto.

What I have learned or had reconfirmed in all of this is a simple lesson—give young people a decent education and a warm, healthy environment in which to learn, *and* they will flourish; they will be more inclined to choose creation over destruction; kindness over meanness; active productivity over passive inactivity. Most young people want to do well; sadly—as Jonathan Kozol writes, "we soil them needlessly." At Crossroads, we have learned how not to soil children, and how to help them do their best. It isn't that difficult.

Note

A collection of newspaper and magazine articles, brochures, and video tapes are available from Michele Hickey, Director, Office of Community Relations, Crossroads School, 1714 21st Street, Santa Monica, California, 90404; (310) 829-7391.

Chapter 11

Independent Schools:
Institutional Community Service—
A New Opportunity

Before I built a wall I'd ask to know
What I was walling in or walling out,
And to whom I was like to give offense.
                    —Robert Frost, "Mending Wall"

It is either the beginning or the end
of the world, and the choice is ourselves
or nothing.

                              —Carolyn Forché

The Garden and the Forest Fire

About five years ago I decided that I knew very little about public education. So, one day, pretty much on a whim, I picked up the phone and began contacting principals at public schools, conveying my desire to visit and learn. The outcome was that I visited seven schools and went back or had return visits to my school from four of the seven principals with whom I felt a particular openness. In several cases, now five years later, we have established friendships which go beyond our professional relationships. We have also designed several joint ventures which I will discuss later. But, most importantly, we have broken down several walls.

For me, the visits to public schools were an eye-opener. Personal contact led me to read more, become involved in two statewide educational projects (California Leadership and the

California Alliance for Arts Education) and, now, to proselytize for greater private school involvement in public education. Why this new effort? Simply because our societal crisis cuts across such artificial distinctions as public or private; there are crises and tragedies which affect us all, and they cannot be solved by the *haves* retreating behind walls and shutting themselves off from the *have-nots*. Furthermore, the walls can no longer be built high enough to protect anyone from a *dis*integrating society. Muggings, crime, drive-by shootings, senseless violence now spill all over the city—nowhere is one completely safe. As Willy Loman says in *Death of a Salesman*, "the woods are burning, boys."

A friend of mine, Mike Babcock, who is the headmaster of Pasadena Polytechnic School in Pasadena, California, recently had a dream which he recounted at a small gathering of heads of private schools. In his dream, he was tending his well-manicured garden, trimming and weeding here and there, and watering a bit. Nearby, there was a superhighway dividing his garden from an immense overgrown forest. As he was tending his beautiful small garden, he noticed the forest was engulfed in a wild, raging forest fire. What should he do? Continue to tend his garden, or take his hose across the highway and try to help put out the fire? We all agreed that his dream captured the dilemma of those of us in private education. Should we turn our backs on the public woods that are burning and simply continue to tend our pretty little gardens?

The dilemma is, of course, insoluble, but I would argue that while we tend to our gardens, we must also help to put out the raging forest fire. But first, what is the nature of the fire?

Well, look at the list of what most public schools have to contend with:

- Budget cuts
- Program cuts
- Overcrowded classrooms
- Drop-outs
- Crime, gangs, violence, guns
- Drugs
- Teenage pregnancies
- Teenage suicides
- Homeless children

- Immigrant children (100 languages in California public schools)
- Segregated schools
- Children from broken (most often single mother only) families
- Abused, malnourished, and neglected children

These are, for the most part, *not* the problems of private-prep schools. Emerging out of this list of major problems is perhaps the most devastating result of all—a generation of angry, alienated, and hopeless young people.

One of the horrible things we have all let happen is for our children to receive *less* than we were given as children. We have cut the heart out of the education program, and the result is children and teenagers who are disengaged from the whole process. For example, cutting the arts out of public education is, I believe, a major tragedy. The arts are a prime place where children can express something of their own uniqueness, where they can say something about their feelings, their inner life. But, because of the funding crisis in public education, arts programs have been decimated and in many school districts have all but disappeared. Initially, our children are the victims, but in the long (and even in the short) run, we are all victims. For the loss of the arts impoverishes us all and releases onto the streets a generation of young people with underdeveloped values, underdeveloped sensitivities, and a lack of understanding of the spiritual dimension of life. As C.S. Lewis wrote, "we castrate and bid the geldings be fruitful."

Two First Steps to Regenerate Schools

What then are we to do? I have two sets of suggestions. One set is on a larger scale and the second is on a smaller scale. On the larger scale, there are *two* immediate steps we could take to regenerate our public schools:

- Cut class size in half
- Restore or create programs which engage children in the arts; environmental education; community service; human development.

This would, of course, be enormously expensive; it would more than double the public school budgets. Where might the money come from?

There are many possible sources for funding (which I outline in chapters 16 and 17), but we must first accept the need for drastically rejuvenating our schools. Private industry and businesses—large and small—will need to play a major role. It is in everyone's best interests to do so.

Furthermore, I would urge private school trustees and executives to reevaluate several clichés commonly used in discussions about what is wrong in public education:

Cliché #1–Waste and mismanagement is the problem;
Cliché #2–Adequate funds are available.

My experience over the years convinces me that *neither* proposition is true. The schools are, in fact, overcrowded, underfunded, and underprogrammed. Furthermore, each year they are being asked to cope with new and escalating social problems. For example, at the very moment in California history when we have cut public education funding, we are experiencing a rapid rise of immigrant enrollment and of homeless children, of gangs and campus violence, and the like. Many public school teachers and administrators, are doing a heroic job coping. It is *we* who have let them down. The problem is not waste; the problem is a lack of funds to do the job properly.

On the second front, the smaller scale of our individual private schools, I would argue that each of our schools has its own unique resources to share with local public schools. I will tell you what our school, Crossroads School, has done—partially because I am proud of our accomplishments, but primarily to offer an example of the kinds of things that the private sector can do.

Public/Private Collaboration

Having made my first phone call and first visits to several public schools, I set about a second round of visits. At one, Palms Middle School, I asked the vice principal, Lana Brody (a dynamic educator), if there was anything my school could do to help her. It was a casual question which, in retrospect, changed my life. She said, "Oh, yes. You do the arts so well; we would love a choral program." I responded, "That's easy, we'll loan you our teacher two hours a week." So, initially, Crossroads School paid its choral teacher, Thea Kano, to teach two hours a week at this public school. The public school was thrilled; eighty children showed up at the tryouts and soon a functioning after-school chorus was performing for the entire community. Subsequently, Crossroads secured a small grant to support the chorus, which then expanded to two groups—a during-class-hours group and an after-school group. This process opened my eyes. What do private schools do well? Answer: we fund-raise. That is, we have funding resources unavailable to most public schools. Why not share them?

So next I went to musician Herb Alpert (a co-founder of A&M Records and the founder of an enlightened and proactive foundation), and Kip Cohen, the president and executive director of The Herb Alpert Foundation, and explained my idea. The idea was to put the arts back into public schools through the support of private funds. Herb, his wife, Lanie, and Kip were excited by the idea, and the Herb Alpert Foundation then pledged a three-year grant of $600,000 to fund music, visual arts, dance, and drama at one public elementary school. We selected Broadway Elementary School—a low-income, 90 percent Hispanic school. The school's morale was as low as could be, and several teachers were planning to quit or take early retirement. Without overstating the case, the infusion of arts into the school was a joy for all. Every child received music, art, dance, and drama—every week—all year, at all grade levels. The halls came alive with children's art, with murals, with the sounds of music and dance. One teacher withdrew her resignation, another canceled her early retirement plans. The children, starved for opportunities for self-expression, were fed the arts and responded with enthusiasm. Now, five years later, many have gone on in middle school to continue their studies in the arts. According to Broadway School's dedicated principal, Ed Romotski, the school—which recently received a campus clean-up grant from the Sterling Foundation—has regained a sense of pride.

After launching the Herb Alpert/Broadway program, we then set out to do the same at a nearby school. Coeur d'Alene

Elementary School is equally poor but more racially mixed than Broadway. It also has the additional problem of being identified as a school for homeless and immigrant children. It too had virtually no programs in the arts when we suggested in 1991-92 providing them with a Broadway School-type program. The principal, Beth Ojena, an extraordinary leader, was thrilled with the idea. Soon, we received foundation support for Coeur d'Alene from visionary foundations such as the Dougherty Foundation, the Barbra Streisand Foundation, the Heller Financial Group, the Roth Family Foundation, the Plum Foundation, and the Los Angeles Cultural Affairs Division. We then launched a comprehensive program at Coeur d'Alene in September of 1993.

Since then, the same transformation has taken place at Coeur d'Alene. Teachers were inspired, parents thrilled, and children were delighted. The growth of school pride was reflected in 1995 when the school received a Redbook Award as one of the 140 finest elementary schools in the country. Principal Ojena credits the arts program with being a major factor in that award.

Expanding Public/Private Collaboration

Thus, with two comprehensive programs and a choral program in place, I realized that a whole new adventure was unfolding—one which needed ongoing funding. So, with the blessings of the Crossroads School board of trustees, we created a separate nonprofit foundation—the Crossroads Community Foundation (CCF). The CCF set as its mission the funding of Broadway, Coeur d'Alene, and a new project—setting up after-school programs in music, art, dance and drama at a local boys/girls club (the Santa Monica Boys/Girls Club).

The CCF began with an annual budget of $150,000—primarily to pay the salaries of arts teachers who are then "loaned" to the public schools and the boys/girls club. That budget has now grown to $450,000 for 1996-97 and three new schools have been added to the CCF mission: one middle school and two new elementary schools. Venice, California, is a diverse, racially mixed community with a complex of fourteen Los Angeles Unified Schools in its area. The CCF now funds arts programs in six of the fourteen schools. Its goal is to add the other eight to its mission and to seek funding from the record and entertainment industry. In addition to funding arts programs at six public schools, Crossroads School is also helping fund a human development program at a local middle school.

Given all of this activity, and given the increasing fundraising demands, the Crossroads board of trustees voted to create a new position, president of the school, to allow me to focus my attention on long-range plans and fundraising for Crossroads, and fundraising and direction for the CCF. Roger Weaver, my ten-year partner and associate headmaster of Crossroads, became headmaster. In making this commitment, the board was acknowledging the importance of the private sector's partnership with, and support of, the public sector.

In September of 1995, we launched yet another outreach program—the creation of a new school. First—and again with the Crossroads School board's blessings—another foundation was established: the New Visions Foundation. Its goal is to establish new schools which are racially diverse (with a minimum of 40 percent students of color), small and academically rigorous, with 100 percent of the students targeted for college admissions. The first of these new schools, New Roads Middle School, began in September 1995 with grades 6–8 (70 students, 52 percent students of color) and will expand to a full 6–12 school. The second New Roads School campus opened in September of 1997 in Baldwin Hills, a diverse neighborhood in central Los Angeles with a large African-American population. And, a third campus for grades 9–10 opened in September of 1997. The New Visions Foundation hopes to start several such schools in the Los Angeles area.

To summarize, Crossroads School (in addition to establishing community service as a graduation requirement for all of its students) has developed a relatively new concept of institutional community service. We believe that institutions themselves should be models of what they expect their students to do. The pay-offs, we believe, are manifold: our students graduate with a deep awareness of community needs, public school children receive programs they would not otherwise receive, more teachers are employed, and public school children begin to see the potential career opportunities available in the arts. In turn, we fully expect to see fewer dropouts, fewer angry, alienated youths.

Chapter 12

The Quest for Unity:
One Language, Many Stories

Nothing is so hard as to understand that there are human
beings in this world beside one's self and one's set.
—William Dean Howells (1872)

I will tell you something about stories . . . they aren't
just entertainment. Don't be fooled.
—Leslie Marmon Silko

Recently, I heard a noted demographer state that the United
States is undergoing the most dramatic cultural and demographic shift in its history, and many cities (for example, Los
Angeles) are undergoing demographic shifts as great as any in
the history of humankind. Yet, while these two statements may
be true, they contain a disturbing distortion. I believe the man
who made this statement overlooked at least two other startling demographic shifts. And his overlooking is indicative, in
a profound way, of a serious problem we are all wrestling with
today.

Whose Demographic Shift?

The current demographic shift is seen from the perspective of
a white male scholar, acknowledging a changing reality for
white citizens. Demographers estimate, for example, that one
half of births in 2025 will be nonwhite, and that half of the
United States population will be nonwhite by 2050. This strikes
fear in the hearts of many whites, particularly among those of

the so-called religious right and more conservative whites in general. The European Protestant culture is strongly ingrained in these groups and has always been more concerned with racial homogeneity than even the Catholic Europeans. In addition, whites in this country have taken racial privilege and power for granted for centuries and now are finding that privilege challenged. It may even be that there is an unconscious fear on the part of the current white "majority" that when they themselves become a minority, they will receive the same kind of prejudicial treatment they have meted out for centuries. Yet, let us backtrack to 1492 when America was a land populated exclusively by nonwhite natives. The demographic shift—more accurately described as the extermination of the Indians—was an even more dramatic, revolutionary shift in population. In 1492, prior to Columbus's landing at the island of Hispaniola, there were some 8 million people—whom he came to name Indians—living there. In twenty-one years, Hispaniola was virtually desolate. Nearly 8 million people had been killed by violence, disease, and despair. And, Hispaniola was merely the start of it all. During the next four hundred years, the aggression of the Europeans and the continuation of violence by the Americans led to the death of as many as 100 million native people.[1] It was the most staggering and massive process of genocide in the history of the world. This "shift" somehow is ignored by many of the fearful today, no doubt because it happened to "them," not to "us."

A similar shift occurred in the seventeenth century in "The New World," both before and after America became a nation. The sudden importation of African slaves was yet another major population shift. It is, however, not considered as such since, again, for white demographers the shift occurred for "them" (each of whom was initially regarded as 3/5 a person by the framers of the Constitution) and not "us."

Now, in the 1990s, many white citizens are bemoaning the changing population patterns. The criticism takes the form of opposing even legal immigration or political correctness, or multiculturalism as un-American separatism, but these arguments, I believe, conceal a deeper fear. It is the fear of intermingling or intermarrying with people who don't look like "us." Their lips are thicker, or their eyes are shaped more narrowly, or their hair is thicker, or whatever. They don't look like what white Americans think Americans should look like.

The sad irony is that the new immigrants have come here for the same reasons that European settlers came here throughout the 1600s–1900s: the quest for a new Eden. Their search comes from the same deep motivation: hope for the future. It is here where the various demographic shifts can be analyzed and celebrated—the human need for hope. This is where "Americans" can find the unity so many citizens desire. The paths in quest of the prize are varied and exciting, and each has a piece of the glory that could be American. But the prize is the same—hope and freedom and opportunity. Change of the magnitude that is occurring in America today is clearly fraught with danger, but it also holds out great possibilities. This is the subject matter our schools should be examining: both the dangers and the possibilities.

Multiculturalism and Separatism

Curiously, one finds today that nonwhite separatists are re-adopting arguments from the 1896 *Plessy v. Fegusson* Supreme Court decision affirming that separate can be equal. They also argue that integrated schools leads inevitably to a diluted culture and traditions of nonwhite groups. And, from white separatists we find several arguments (ranging from the rational to the bigoted) against diversity: (a) that forced integration leads to ill will and conflict; (b) that a superior European culture is diluted by the inclusion of "lesser" cultures in the curricula; (c) that integrated studying will inevitably lead to intermarriage and the contamination of pure blood; (d) that studying other cultures will lead to the devaluation of white European standards as the yardstick by which all cultures should be measured.

Having acknowledged that there are both whites and nonwhites who argue in favor of educational and cultural separatism, and while I agree with the goal of preservation which some of these separatists advocate, I cannot agree with their means. First of all, separatism is a political and economic impossibility on a purely practical level. The peoples and cultures of America are so inextricably intertwined, there can be no going back to a day when the various groupings were apart. Furthermore, given the economic disparities which exist, and are even widening, between the white power structure, on the one hand, and the poorer "minorities" on the other, to insist upon separate expressions of differences without seeking unifying processes will simply mean that the white elites will celebrate their differences in relative wealth while the majority of the nonwhites will celebrate their differences in poverty.

The dangers of separatist multiculturalism have been outlined in several books, perhaps most notably (since it appeared to be a betrayal of liberalism by one of its staunch advocates) by Arthur Schlesinger, Jr. in his extended essay, *The Disuniting of America: Reflections on a Multicultural Society*. Schlesinger made himself somewhat unpopular by asking questions many would have rather left unasked. For example:

> Watching ethnic conflict tear one nation after another apart, one cannot look with complacency at proposals to divide the United States into distinct and immutable ethnic and racial communities, each taught to cherish its own apartness from the rest. One wonders: will the center hold? Or will the melting pot give way to the tower of Babel?"
> (Schlesinger, 1992: 18)

Schlesinger continues by suggesting that what began as an ethnic awakening and a protest against Eurocentrism has become a cult which today "threatens to become a counter revolution against the original theory of America as 'one people', a common culture, a single nation" (1992: 43). While acknowledging that history books have too long neglected racial minorities, Schlesinger fears that they are now becoming places where minorities embrace group identities and promote self-esteem rather than presenting the story of a single nation.

The kind of separation which Schlesinger and others fear is, certainly, understandable. The city in which I live, Los Angeles, is a vivid example of racial, ethnic, and class separation. There is a Chinatown, Korea Town, 'Little Vietnam'; segregated schools are the norm; there are over ninety newspapers in different languages; there are ballots in different languages; a given public school may find up to forty to fifty different, non-English first languages spoken, and so on. Moreover, gangs stake out strict geographic territories and woe be to anyone who unwittingly strays into such areas. And across town—West Los Angeles—white people live in fancy homes, purchase private security patrols, reside in walled-in communities, send their children to private schools, and have little exchange with nonwhites. Many have characterized this trend as a retreat to tribalism. The national motto of *E Pluribus Unum*—out of many, one—is seeming less and less a reality or even a possibility.

A second danger of separatism is simply the widening of the gap between the rich and the poor, the haves and have-nots, the white power structure and all others. A recent study from Tufts University reported that "if current trends continue, half of all black and Hispanic children will be poor by 2010" (*Education Week*, November 3, 1993). The director of the study, J. Larry Brown, wrote that "American children are being divided into two separate countries." This, of course, is echoed in the title of Andrew Hacker's important book, *Two Nations: Black and White, Separate, Hostile, Unequal*, which outlines conditions that keep many blacks from experiencing any piece of the American dream. The Tufts report goes on to illustrate that since 1973, the number of poor Latino children has gone up 116 percent. Thus, while one may fervently believe in ethnic pride, it is hard to escape the conclusion that ethnic separatism simply exacerbates an already horrible gulf between races and may even, in fact, be doing the white-power separatists a service. Without a first-rate knowledge of English and a reasonable knowledge of white Eurocentric economics and culture, there is little cause to believe that minorities will escape the miserable cycle of poverty which now persists, generation after generation. So that, while I will argue that the celebration of one's non-European culture is desirable, I will argue equally strongly that all citizens must know something of the nation's European traditions and democratic inheritances. We must also, I believe, forge some new stories, but that is matter for later discussion. In addition, I believe we need to study carefully and in depth the sources and manifestations of right-wing ideologies which, in addition to their religious fundamentalist roots, reflect a strong tradition of paranoia, anti-intellectualism, nativism, and racism.

A third danger of tribalism is simply the loss of enrichment for all. I grew up in a WASP home and subculture. I ate steak and mashed potatoes, listened to George Shearing and Doris Day, my parents attended exclusive country clubs: I attended an all-white private high school. My life was impoverished by its very homogeneity. I was simply oblivious to the diversity of the city. I had never heard of sushi or salsa; my high school American history textbook referred to the extermination of the Native Americans as *our* "manifest destiny." There was not a single black or Asian student in my graduating class. I was, in short, culturally deprived. That same kind of deprivation threatens to return (in some cases) or be extended (in others) if American citizens allow separatism to rule the day. *E Pluribus Unum* is, I believe, still a worthy motto, but, it is endangered from the left and from the right. As we have seen, on the so-called left, minorities themselves seek an ethnic and racial identity separate from a national identity. On the right we are witnessing a regressive attack against so-called multiculturalism, a distrust and fear of nonwhites which has strong racial antecedents.

To pause and summarize for a moment: we see that the United States is experiencing a dramatic demographic shift from a white European majority to a nonwhite, non-European majority and that, concurrently, the nation is in danger of becoming less unified, with ethnic and racial groups going their separate ways. Both of these possibilities have triggered a backlash against multiculturalism which manifests itself in several ways.

The Backlash against Multiculturalism

Let us look at some of these reactions. One writer even refers to our end of century period as a time of "culture wars in the United States" (Takaki, 1989: 276-299). Part of the backlash has come from conservative critics of multiculturalism, which is portrayed as a threat to the social fabric of America. Thus, at the 1992 Republican convention, Pat Buchanan urged his fellow Republicans to take back "our" culture, "our" cities, "our" country. In this context, presumably "our" meant "we whites," and "them" would, therefore, be nonwhites. It is, however, hard to understand in what ways the white power structure has surrendered any real power to nonwhites. What Buchanan was probably expressing was a vague, racist feeling or perhaps a fear of becoming the nonmajority race. Others have been more subtle than Buchanan and have tried to denigrate cultural pluralism by linking it to silly excesses of political correctness. It is an old yet effective technique: tarnish an enlightened movement by exaggerating trivial blemishes within the movement. In addition to using this technique, other writers have simply appealed to a kind of cultural jingoism of whites by suggesting that if curricula are expanded to include nonwhite authors, then white writers will cease to be read. Thus, if we assign Langston Hughes, then somehow no one will ever read Robert Frost. Schlesinger, a good old-fashioned liberal in his day, seems quite concerned that by exaggerating ethnic differences, we will be driving "ever deeper the awful wedges between races" (quoted in Takaki, 1989: 297). Yet, as Ron Takaki points out, in one of Schlesinger's own major works, *The Age of Jackson*, "there is no mention of two marker events—the Nat Turner insurrection and Indian Removal, which Andrew Jackson himself would have been surprised to find omitted from a history of his era" (Takaki, 1989: 297). The explanation for this, I believe, is easy to see: when Schlesinger wrote his book in 1945, racial and ethnic fairness was not a conscious concern of most historians.

I attended Stanford University from 1955–1959 and as an American history major never read of, heard a lecture about, or discussed in class the holocaust that occurred in this country—the virtual extermination of the Native Americans. Then, I took a year-long class from Arthur Schlesinger, Jr., 1959–60, at Harvard with the same result. It wasn't until the 1960s' civil rights movements and thereafter that this kind of awareness penetrated the universities—let alone the society at large. Even now, Schlesinger and other critics of multiculturalism see a threat in the desire of others to tell a comprehensive story of America. They see a danger of an exaggeration of ethnic differences. But, one must ask, is it an exaggeration to tell the truth? If the story of the founding fathers used to be accorded ten pages in a history text, and now is accorded only five, then some see a diminution of *the* story. But, if you see the story as composed of multiple stories, then restoring lost and neglected accounts of other Americans is not a diminution; it is an expansion of the story. America has always been a nation of new peoples. Today is no different—they (the new) only look different. Their dreams and visions are as old as the founding of the nation.

Along with a conservative backlash have come other unfortunate reactions to multicultural pressures. We see an increase in racism, antisemitism, and antifeminism across the country. Generally speaking, such reactions of hatred and violence are the expressions of fear, fear of too rapid change. We also see the media fanning the flames of fear by reporting almost exclusively violent crimes of blacks and browns rather than their acts of kindness, community-building, and positive contributions to society. Consequently, when many whites see black or brown people, they react with suspicion and fear; they move out of their homes when blacks reach 10 percent of the neighborhood; they seek all-white schools and avoid social interactions with blacks and browns. Finally, they are willing to allow blacks and browns to live in squalid conditions which they would find utterly intolerable for their own children. This insensitivity, of course, propels people of color to seek their separate racial identities—what choice do they have?

Toward a More Pluralistic, Harmonious Nation

I would like to be so presumptuous as to propose several prescriptions for a more pluralistic and harmonious nation. The ideal of the melting pot—of melting diversity down to a single, homogeneous soup—is no longer tenable even if it were desirable—which few today would advocate. The more likely and exciting prospect is the creation of a new society in which separate cultural identities are preserved while at the same time each becomes a strand in a new tapestry—a pluralistic nation in which diverse stories and values are shared. This presumes communication between all the different cultural, ethnic, and international identities which would comprise this new America. It would also presume a common language—English. Thus, while I would argue for the necessity of each separate group to preserve its own language (how else could it preserve its stories?), I would argue equally strongly that each child *master* English. By master I mean achieve fluency, comfort, and complexity of expression—both written and spoken. If we cannot educate all children in our common language, the opponents of multiculturalism will have a field day. The charges against multiculturalism of divisiveness, fragmentation, geographic and cultural isolation, exclusionism, the loss of a common heritage—all these and more—will be forcefully disseminated. The only way multiculturalism will achieve productive acceptance is if all children learn English. Already, multiculturalism and multilingualism are regarded with suspicion and, often, outright hostility. White citizens and civic leaders see their country changing under their very eyes. In California, Texas, Illinois, Florida, and New York, the changes have been unprecedented. Thus, a retrenchment into "good old-fashioned American values" is to be expected. But the conservative approach, if modified by intelligent liberalism, can lead to mutually desired results.

Thus, first of all, I would argue for the continuation of a bilingual acclimatization for immigrant children with the understanding that their native language is not only an end in itself, but is the principal means of leading that student to a mastery of English. Simply dropping a non–English-speaking immigrant student into an all-English-speaking class is unrealistic and unfair. Some explanation in one's native language is necessary to bridge the gap.

Second, I would argue that increased funds be raised (see chapters 16 and 17) in order to reduce class size; to provide teacher training and enrichment; and to hire more qualified teachers of *English*. One reason why both bilingualism and monolingualism (English) are not effective is the same as why math, science, and history teachers are ineffective. It has nothing to do with the subject—it has everything to do with class size, teaching conditions, neighborhood deterioration, and the like. We cannot put forty non–English-speaking students in an English class and expect much progress. So, one way to improve students' English skills is simply to adopt sensible reform of intolerable teaching conditions—for all subjects.

Third, I suggest that we provide at least one year of intensive English for non–English-speaking students. One year. Six hours-a-day. Will this be costly? Yes and no. The costs can be mitigated by postponing—for one year—instruction of other subjects and simply focusing on English. In the long run, a student who speaks and writes English well is more likely to do well in school, not to drop out, not to join the ranks of the alienated, and, hence, less likely to join gangs, engage in criminal activities, and finally, become part of the incredibly costly prison system. Let's assume for the moment that we as a nation are dedicated to improving classroom, including English-language–teaching conditions. Given that assumption, what further steps would we need to take to create a *United* States, a unified yet pluralistic nation? We would need to expand our teaching of history to be the teaching of histories. Certainly the story of the white European colonists, the white male leaders of the Revolution, the framers of the Constitution, and the captains of industry, inventors, foreign adventurers, and others is an essential piece of American history. But it is not the whole story. It omits the stories of women, as told by, experienced by, interpreted by, and written by women. The white European male story also omits the Native American stories; the stories of Spanish and Mexican settlers and immigrants; the stories of Chinese laborers and other Asian immigrants: and, of course it omits the stories of African-American slaves and the subsequent stories of blacks in America. Each of these stories is interdependent with the others. A rich fusion of music, art, political aspiration and achievement, intermarriage, conflict, injustices and triumphs—they are all part of a New Story we could as a nation recreate and create. The Baha'i faith proclaims that the earth is but one country, and mankind its citizens. It would be a stunning achievement if the United States of America were able to adopt this principle within its own borders.

Fourth, and finally, I do not believe that a common language and an inclusive sense of histories are by themselves enough to achieve a united country. There is another piece (discussed in chapter 14) which is essential: we cannot achieve unity if our schools and neighborhoods remain segregated, and segregated with "savage inequalities." The next generation of citizens and leaders will not and cannot find the means to communicate and to create community if they remain apart in rich enclaves and poor ghettoes attending segregated schools which, for the vast majority of minority children, means being relegated to underfunded, dilapidated, wholly inadequate schools.

So, again, we see the interrelationship of all of our educational and social problems. In this case, multiculturalism is not a villain, but a blessing waiting to be received. The real villains are poverty, greed, selfishness, insensitivity, fear, exclusivity, xenophobia, racism, snobbery, elitism, and the like. Children are not naturally inclined to this sad and sorry list. We teach them to be so. What a thrilling prospect it would be, just once, to teach a generation of children to respect and honor differences, to welcome change, and to seek to create newer and richer histories of America.

Note

1 These and other equally shocking statistics are available in sources such as: Howard Zinn, 1992, and David E. Stannard, 1992.

Chapter 13

Gender Issues: She, He, and We

Written by Anna K. Cummins

How does a woman gain a sense of her self in a system which devalues work done by women?

—Adrienne Rich

There is no savor
More sweet, more salt
Than to be glad to be
What, woman,
And who, myself,
I am, a shadow
That grows longer as the sun
moves, drawn out
on a thread of wonder.

—Denise Levertov

Part of the Problem

At recess, the boys congregate outside to play a violent game of "butts up," which involves repeatedly punching the loser, while the girls are huddled in groups inside, comparing outfits, whispering and giggling, applying lipstick and hairspray in the bathroom.

In a discussion about homosexuality, the boys wonder why girls sometimes "act like lesbians," holding hands, linking arms, hugging and "carrying on," while the girls wonder why boys are so afraid to show affection toward one another, to cry, or even to have such a discussion at all without "turning it into a big joke."

While these are actual events that I have witnessed at the school where I work, they could describe any junior high or high school in America. Are we, as men and women, really so different from one another that we naturally evolve toward such cliched stereotypes as the ones described above? Or have we thus far been unable to overcome an extreme cultural/societal ignorance of the opposite sex, and continue to pass this ignorance on to our children?

Today, we live in a culture which is still highly polarized along the lines of gender. Although we have made marked improvement in broaching the barriers between men's monopoly over the public sphere of society and women's confinement to the private sphere, evidence abounds of our continuing ignorance regarding gender equity. One cannot open a newspaper without seeing examples of this ignorance staring us in the face: crimes of brutality against women, prepubescent, anorexic girls glorified as ideals of female beauty, soaring statistics of male homicide, the preponderance of men over women in the most costly and prestigious college programs, marked inequalities in men's and women's salaries, a conspicuous absence of female political leaders, and so on.

These problems will not disappear, and will only become magnified, unless we begin educating our children with more enlightened classes and programs than perhaps we ourselves were given. Schools are supposedly the institutions where children are to be equipped with the academic and social tools which will best prepare them to be healthy, productive citizens, active in trying to bring about positive contributions to society. However, in our schools, we are failing to teach one of the most fundamental human skills: how to respect, cohabitate, work with, and understand, in short, how to deal with the opposite sex. And we are paying a heavy price for this failure.

The question of whether or not men and women are born with certain innate, biologically based personality differences is a highly complex, controversial topic. I do not claim to have

the answer, but rather to examine the ways in which our schools, and by extension, society, serve to widen and accentuate these differences, whether they be the result of genetics, socialization, or most likely, a combination of the two. Nor do I wish to suggest that we should seek to deny or eliminate any and all differences between the sexes, but rather to study them, talk about them, and in doing so, try to have a better understanding of their impact upon us.

Recently, the issue of how gender plays a role in young people's access to an equal education has come to greater public attention. Statistics from a 1992 American Association of University Women (*The AAUW Report*) show a significant disparity between testing scores, self-esteem, and academic confidence of adolescent boys and girls. A host of books have been written on the topic (see Further Reading), familiarizing us with the most common gender-related problems in schools: females are *not* being encouraged to pursue higher-level math and science courses, are *not* being given the same support in athletics as boys, are *not* performing as well on the standardized tests necessary for acceptance in universities and graduate school, and are *not* receiving the same confidence-building experience of studying themselves in their curriculum. And yet they *are* attending the same schools!

Invisible Schoolgirls
Our traditional teaching methods are furthering cycles of gender inequity in the classroom and beyond. I refer here to the standard classroom structure of lecture/absorption: the teacher stands at the blackboard disseminating information, while the students passively absorb the material. When students are called on, the male students overwhelmingly dominate, monopolizing the teacher's time and energy. The underlying message imparted to female students by this common classroom scenario is that their place is to be silent and passive, allowing the boys to take full advantage of the opportunities and resources being offered, while they are denied recognition from their primary academic resource and authority figure, the teacher. This syndrome of the silent schoolgirl is one of the most common, recurrent themes related to gender inequity in

schools. The denial of this basic classroom privilege, recognition, is in turn responsible for a host of other related inequalities.

Not only are girls given markedly less attention in the classroom; compared to boys, the quality and content of the attention given to girls is also unequal. Teachers tend to respond to girls' comments with, "O.K." "Fine," or "Mm-hm" while giving the boys much more extensive feedback: encouraging them when they are wrong, challenging them to develop their thoughts, and strongly praising them when they are correct (Brophy, cited in *The AAUW Report*, 1992: 119–120). In addition, female students tend to receive much more positive feedback than males do about their physical appearance, something both out of their control and irrelevant to their intellectual capacities—thereby reinforcing the notion that beauty rather than brains is the ideal to strive for (Sadker and Sadker, 1994: 56).

In witnessing the dynamics in a number of classes as a student and a teacher, I have seen this same pattern time and time again: when student input is requested, the boys frantically wave their hands, accompanying their dramatic hand gestures with insistent whining and groaning noises, while the girls seem to shrink into their seats and turn invisible. Ironically, when the boys are called on, often they have missed the question, so intent are they on ensuring that their voice is heard. Or in other cases, they simply have the wrong answer, showing little or none of the mortification that girls show when they hazard a wrong answer.

In *Failing at Fairness*, the Sadkers speak of a pattern where girls who are identified as highly intelligent and capable display extreme insecurity about their talents and downplay their achievements. When complimented, these girls tend to make excuses for their successes much more than boys of equal or lesser abilities (1994: 90–91). Where their male counterparts will exhibit confidence in their achievements, girls will often apologize for them with comments like, "Oh, it must have been an easy exam" or "Oh, the teacher was just being nice."

As these same girls grow older, this behavior translates into an extreme lack of confidence in their skills, and a ready deferment of initiative to males who in some cases are less qualified, but yet are more comfortable with assertiveness. Women who have been highly educated and have excelled in academic performance statistically have a much higher likelihood to doubt their abilities, attributing them to luck rather than merit. At the same time, the patterns learned by boys early in life to shout out to be heard lead in adulthood to an ease and comfort with those qualities necessary in positions of leadership and authority: trusting in one's opinions, delegating responsibility, and taking control.

Self-Esteem

Numerous studies on patterns of educational development throughout elementary and high school indicate that at the elementary level, girls consistently outperform boys in many areas of the curriculum, including math and science (Mullis, cited in Sadker, 1994: 291). Yet somewhere around middle school, in conjunction with an overall decline in adolescent girls' self-esteem, their academic performance begins to drop as well. While problems with self-esteem are not exclusive to women, there is nonetheless overwhelming evidence that girls are more prone to negative conceptions of self. In the 1992 *The AAUW Report*, an average of 69 percent of elementary school boys, and 60 percent of girls described themselves as "happy the way I am." In high school, the numbers for both sexes decrease, to 46 percent, for boys, and 29 percent for girls (1992: 19). What is happening at this point in young women's lives to account for this systematic decline in their confidence and productivity?

It is around these very years, twelve to eighteen, that adolescents begin going through enormous physical and emotional transformations. We as a society do little to prepare them for these changes, nor do we provide any rites of passage. At the same time that young girls begin this crucial transformation, typically a time when young people struggle and search for their sense of identity, girls find that women's issues are conspicuously absent from the school curriculum. As an African-American senior from New York describes her experience, "In twelve years of school, I never studied anything about myself" (*AAUW*, 1992: 105). As girls begin to look outward for role models in the texts they study, the leaders they are taught to admire, and the career opportunities which are associated with power, authority, and economic success, the reflections of men are overwhelmingly mirrored back at them.

Media Influence

At a very young age, girls have already learned that they do not have unlimited access to all avenues of society, and that to an extent, their gender is defined by what they *can't* or *shouldn't* do. In *Schoolgirls*, Peggy Orenstein describes a classroom experiment which illustrates the damaging effect these messages have on young children. In this experiment, a sixth-grade teacher asks her classroom to imagine that they were born the opposite sex, and to make a list of everything that would be different about their lives thus far. When the students read their lists out loud, everything the boy listed began, "I would have to . . ." (I would have to worry about getting pregnant, I would have to stand around at recess instead of getting to play, I would have to help cook, etc.) whereas the girls' examples were phrased in terms of what they would "get to do." (I would get to play more sports, I would get to stay out later, I would get to dress however I wanted, etc.) (Orenstein, 1994: xi–xv). Thus they have already learned to envision their gender as characterized by limitations, while viewing the opposite sex as free of restrictions.

In addition, in an age where television has replaced reading and playing for many children, the void that we create by failing to provide young people with positive gender models, and by excluding gender issues from the curriculum of our schools, is filled by a host of extremely damaging gender stereotypes. Children are barraged with constant exposure to films, magazines, and other media of popular culture which glorify male aggression, female subservience, and which depict women as sex objects. By not helping elementary and high school students begin to face the consequences and issues of their emerging sexuality, we are forcing them to rely on these media influences as their models for adult behavior.

Is it any wonder that in the absence of enlightened guidance, boys learn that power and authority are their birthright, while young girls learn that their proper role is to allow boys to take the initiative in matters of leadership and authority, and that their primary value lies in their physical attractiveness? While both boys and girls go through difficult developments throughout elementary and high school, girls' experiences in the classroom teach them to undervalue their academic abilities, one of the most tangible areas in which adolescents learn to measure their self-worth. Confusion regarding their sense of belonging as members of an intellectual institution and their perceived failure to live up to societal ideals of physical perfection contribute to a dramatic plummet in their overall self-esteem.

Hidden Sexism

As Myra and David Sadker discuss in *Failing at Fairness*, much of the sexism occurring in classrooms is hidden, often so subtly that it is easily overlooked by the untrained eye. One of the methods the Sadkers used to document this hidden favoritism was to videotape class sessions, and then analyze the classroom dynamics. In reviewing the footage afterward, many teachers were surprised to find that while they believed they had conducted a relatively fair class, they in fact had virtually ignored the girls (calling on boys at least twice as often), had provided boys with constructive criticism where girls received none, and had encouraged boys to be active and aggressive while leaving the girls unnoticed (Sadker and Sadker, 1994: 42–75).

Even more alarming than this unconscious gender bias is the problem of teachers who consider themselves to be aware of the problem of males dominating the classroom yet who still find themselves unable to prevent it. In study after study, teachers speak of the extreme difficulty they have giving equal attention to female students, even when they are trying to avoid falling into the familiar gender pitfalls. While aware of the consequences of leaving girls unrecognized, many teachers claim they are forced to pander to the behavioral disruptiveness of the boys. As one teacher admits in *Schoolgirls*, "I definitely play to the boys. I know I do. The squeaky wheel gets the grease, and they're louder" (Orenstein, 1994: 29). By constantly ceding to the boys and giving them the attention they demand, teachers inadvertently reward boys for being aggressive, reinforcing their tendencies toward outspokenness, while the girls are taught to be passive and silent.

Part of the Solution

To combat some of the imbalances occurring in classroom after classroom across the country, schools must launch a concerted effort to shift the focus away from the male students, and begin engaging the females in more active learning. At the more basic level, I recommend several specific tactics which can be implemented in the classroom. One such approach was suggested by Ilene Levitt, former president of Middlebury high-school in Vermont. In her ten years as a math teacher, she adopted the strategy of simply calling on students rather than waiting for them to raise their hands or shout out, a format which invariable leads to domination by the boys (Levitt, 1996). By making sure that an equal ratio of boys and girls is called on, this elementary tactic eliminates male monopolization of class time without any radical shift in classroom structure.

Another tactic suggested in *Failing at Fairness* is the use of wait-time by teachers—pausing a few moments in between the time a question is asked and a student is called on to respond, allowing students time to formulate their answers. Studies have shown that female students benefit from being given this extra time, and are more likely to volunteer input when the atmosphere of competition to be the first to shout out is eliminated (Sadker and Sadker, 1994: 57–58).

Teachers can employ such seemingly small yet effective tactics without significantly altering the classroom format. However, for educators willing to depart from the traditional classroom pedagogy, I suggest a more dramatic approach which attempts to address issues of competition v. cooperation, commonly associated with gender. To begin achieving this, schools might implement a more cooperative structure, placing greater emphasis on student participation and initiative. For example, the teacher might direct students to work in small groups, with rotating group leaders, thus allowing both males and females the opportunity to be in positions of responsibility and authority. By encouraging students to work in a more collaborative manner, schools can begin combatting the individualistic, competitive element of our educational system and can help foster the idea in children that the success of the group, and by extension, the community, depends upon equal participation and cooperation. In addition, schools can encourage students to come to more conclusions on their own, rather than merely accepting information from their teacher.

Men's Studies

Giving to girls the full benefit of the educational tools their male peers receive solves only half of the battle. For until we help boys to understand and readapt the damaging gender stereotypes they are burdened with, the problems girls face competing with boys for attention in elementary and high school will become the same problems they will continue to face in secondary school and the working world. In addition, focusing on how girls are victimized and discriminated against gives the impression that this is "a women's problem." As Nina Baym suggests, "to discuss gender as though it pertained to women only is inadvertently to replicate the dangerous cultural fiction that men are not gendered, that they are the disembodied mentality of the human while women are irrevocably embodied in their biological sex: as de Beauvoir put it, 'men equal the transcendent, women the immanent' (Baym, 1992: 57).

While there has been a spate of books regarding girls as victims of gender bias in education and society at large, too little has been written about boys' educational defects and their overall crisis in society. Books such as *Schoolgirls* and *The AAUW Report* have attracted a great deal of attention, and certainly the issues raised in these books of girls being shortchanged warrant serious study and immediate action. But we need to look at how boys are also shortchanged by the culture and their areas of deprivation in schools. For example, there is little discussion in education and societal circles of countercharges such as:

- Boys receive lower grades from elementary through high-school, and are more likely than girls to drop out;
- Boys are nine times more likely to suffer from hyperactivity and high levels of academic stress;
- Boys are three times more likely to become alcohol abusers, and 50 percent more likely to use illicit drugs. Men account for more than 90 percent of alcohol and drug-related arrests;
- Males commit suicide two to three times more often than females (Sadker and Sadker, 1994: 221).

And, in addition to these concerns, there are other ways in which boys suffer in our society. For one, they too are victimized by an outmoded, centuries-old image of men as warriors—that is, those who must wage war. Such images retard their full human development. Second, many boys suffer from the absent-father factor in our society. Certainly girls need a father as well, but more often they at least have a same-sex role model, whereas boys in tragic proportions lack such a model at home and must turn to the mass media for the terminator/delta force/vengeful/kick-ass models of what it means to be male. Being deprived of a strong paternal figure, they are handicapped later in life in not knowing what it means to be a father.

Furthermore, many of the ways in which girls are victims of boys are ways in which boys are themselves victims of destructive acculturation. Little boys who are allowed and even encouraged to tease girls are learning about harassment and abuse, which will ultimately lead them into divorce, jail, or miserable relationships, to say nothing of the continued oppression of women.

For coeducational schools, we suggest a three-part (three-semester or even three-year) human development curriculum of male (boys) and female (girls) studies programs. In part one, the sexes would be separated and each would study classic texts in their respective fields (see Further Reading). In part two, each sex would study the texts and issues of the opposite sex in order to try to see the world as the opposite sex is educated, acculturated, and trained to see it. In part three, the sexes would recombine in small groups to discuss and carry out various activities to bring their new learning into a new dialogue. Single-sex schools might adopt the same approach through part I and part II, and then organize coeducation seminars with opposite, single-sex schools nearby.

An Enormous Task

School should not be envisioned merely as a place to gear students toward standardized tests and college acceptance, but rather as a vital time to begin giving young people the instruments to deal with the ethical decisions and responsibilities they will encounter in the transition to adulthood and as members of a community. To suggest to schools that they take responsibility for transforming the effects of a society which has been under male control for centuries is admittedly an enormous task. Not only must schools battle against the biases and learned prejudices which children are preprogrammed with, but they must take the next step to aid children in finding new models of thinking to promote a more egalitarian society. And few of us may agree what these ways of thinking are. Yet, however daunting it appears, we must at least try to become more aware of the prejudices that our children are unconsciously adopting.

Gender issues, conflicts, and mutually destructive patterns go way beyond the classroom and academic matters to affect boys and girls, men and women, at the deepest emotional and psychic levels. It is not just that the male-dominated society denies women the fullest development of their academic or economic potential—as if this were not destructive enough—it is that both men and women suffer from limiting views of what it means to be a man or a woman. The existing stereotypes are narrow, demeaning to both, and restrict men and women from the separate and mutual joys they might experience if they were not weighed down by conventional, Madison Avenue-fueled, fear-motivated images and modes of behavior.

A few years back, I was given a quote attributed to Gabriel Marquez which offers a startling (that is, to most men) statement that the only hope for humankind in the future was for women to run the world. This full quote is worth examining:

> The only new idea that could save humanity in the twenty-first century is for women to take over the management of the world. I believe that male hegemony has squandered the opportunity of 10,000 years. We men have belittled and ridiculed feminine intuition, and on the other hand, we have historically sanctified our ideologies, almost all of them absurd or abominable. The masculine power structure has proved that it cannot impede the destruction of the environment because it is incapable of overcoming its own interests. For women, on the other hand, the preservation of the environment is a genetic vocation. The reversal of powers is a matter of life and death."[1]

Certainly most people's immediate response will be that this is a quaint idea, but one which has about as much chance as a feather in a whirlwind. Quaint, but hopelessly idealistic. Probably so. Perhaps it would be no more desirable to see the opposite sex totally dominant than to continue with the current male dominance, though it is hard to imagine women doing worse than men have done in ruling. Ultimately, the ideal would be a balance of the masculine and feminine, an equity of power, influence, and opportunity. At present, we are a long way off from such harmony. While it is unlikely that most men will give more than lip service to this ideal, it is worth working toward, for all our sakes.

It seems fair to ask men to try as hard to discover or recover their feminine side as men have required women to do in developing their masculine side, in just about every arena of society. The human race can only benefit if a more harmonious balance is achieved within each individual as well as in society. School is *the* place where imbalances have been taught and reinforced; school can and must be the place where reform begins.

Note

1   We were given this quote of Marquez by a friend. We have been unable to locate its publication. We, therefore, offer it here tentatively as an attribution to Marquez. However, we fully agree with the idea expressed and include it here to stimulate consideration.

—Paul F. Cummins and Anna K. Cummins

INTERDEPENDENCE OF SOCIAL
AND EDUCATIONAL ISSUES

Chapter 14

A Marshall Plan for Black America

The danger of a conflict between the white and
the black inhabitants . . . perpetually haunts the
imagination of the Americans, like a painful dream.
—Alexis de Tocqueville (ca. 1830)

So the question for white Americans is essentially moral:
is it right to impose on members of an entire race a lesser start
in life and then to expect from them a degree of resolution that
has never been demanded from your own race?
—Andrew Hacker (1992)

There are words like liberty
That almost make me cry.
If you had known what I know
You would know why.

—Langston Hughes

When K., a friend of mine, age 33, African-American, drives
with his wife and two children into a gang-infested part of town
where he grew up, he is frequently pulled over by the police.
Often, they draw their guns and point them at his or his wife's
head. Then they see the two children in the back seat and
mutter "You were driving too fast" or "You rolled through a
stop light." But they don't issue a ticket. Nor do they apologize. Why do they stop him (over twenty times last year)? Because he drives a nice car—assumption: he must be a thief or a
drug dealer.

S., a parent at my school, age 35, African-American, tells me
that whenever she enters a department store, the house detec-
tive follows her around. Why? Because it is assumed that since
she is black, she is probably a shoplifter.

I mention these incidents because, though neither is dramatic or life-threatening, they illustrate the sorts of indignities African-American people suffer every day in countless ways in this country. Gunnar Myrdal wrote his classic study, *An American Dilemma: The Negro Problem and Modern Democracy* in 1944, where he concluded "that race in America is essentially a caste condition, so that for all basic purposes, black people never escape their birth" (quoted in Hacker, 1992: xii).

The Failure of Desegregation

Ten years later, the Supreme Court of the United States concluded—in *Brown v. Board of Education*—that in public education the doctrine of "separate but equal" has no place. States and localities were told they could no longer operate schools which divided students by race. It was in many ways a revolutionary decision and it has had a profound impact on the lives of individual black children and families. Anthony Lewis wrote in 1994 (*New York Times*, May 16), that the 1954 decision helped to set in motion a variety of civil rights acts and legislation in the 1960s and eventually helped some children receive a better education—for a time. As James Traub expresses it: "What Brown ordered was the desegregation of the schools; but what it stands for is the hope of redemption from our original sin of slavery and racism" (Traub, 1994: 35). Of course, as Traub continues, "redemption hasn't come." Across the country, desegregation is becoming a dead issue. For example, in Los Angeles, schools throughout the city are hopelessly segregated. Busing has failed to achieve real integration and neighborhoods have become walled apart by the marriage of poverty and race. Some will argue that segregation is merely an unfortunate by-product of economics and poverty. But the correlation between race and poverty is so close that plain common sense suggests that poverty for black America is not an indirect, but a direct result of racism.

Then, as if poverty were not enough to thwart *Brown v. Board of Education*, many states and cities found more direct ways to prevent integration. For example, "In the deep south, eight states passed pupil placement laws designed to block transfers between white schools and black ones, six states authorized the closing of public schools under the threat of integration, four states provided financial aid to students who attended private schools to escape count-ordered desegregation" (White, 1994: 17).

In addition, local school officials found other ways to circumvent or to obstruct integration. These techniques ranged from manipulating attendance zones to building new buildings. They even went so far as "to rezone, rebuild and redevelop the cities in an all-out effort to create barriers between neighborhoods, to isolate black populations, to demolish mixed-race areas, to relocate integrated schools, and otherwise to create an even more segregated society than had existed before Brown" (White, 1994: 18). Meanwhile, northern cities found they could prevent integration by redrawing city boundaries that "reflected the racial characteristics of the neighborhoods rather than the locations of schools" (18). In addition to these actions by states and localities, individual white Americans have taken other actions to avoid integration. Quite simply, they move. According to Andrew Hacker, "Here we have no shortage of studies. By and large, this research agrees that white residents will stay—and some new ones may move in—if black arrivals do not exceed 8 percent. But once the black proportion passes that point, whites begin to leave the neighborhood and no new ones will move in. The vacated houses or apartments will be bought or rented by blacks, and the area will be on its way to becoming all black. What makes integration difficult if not impossible is that so few whites will accept even a racial composition reflecting the overall national proportion of 12 or 13 percent" (Hacker, 1992: 36).

The new result of these actions and of simple poverty combined with a fifteen-year period (1980–1995) of government neglect of the poor has been the death knell of integration. The *Brown v. Board of Education* decision was issued on May 17, 1954, insuring that seven-year-old Linda Brown would attend an integrated school. Forty years later, in 1994, the Topeka schools covered by the original Brown case are still segregated. And across the country, "As U.S. District Judge Robert Carter, who worked on the Brown case, noted in a recent speech, "more black students attend all or virtually all-black schools today than in 1954" (*Nation*, 1994: 88–89). To be more specific, "According to studies by the National School Boards Association, about two-thirds of all black youngsters—63.3 percent—still attend segregated schools" (Hacker, 1992: 162). In large cities where black children are concentrated in segregated sections, the percentage of children attending segregated schools is over 70 percent. Of course, in many of these schools the percent is virtually 100 percent.

Can Segregated Schools Be Equal?

The question which has reasserted itself is, can separate be equal? Some argue that the Brown decision was condescending and even racist. For these people, the new choice, it seems, is between separate but equal and separate but unequal. Segregated schools can offer quality education if we simply provide better facilities, programs and teachers in all-black schools. Separate schools, they argue, are needed to restore black self-esteem and "many blacks now look upon integration as a white plot to undermine racial pride" (Traub, 1994: 36–37). Once again we face the question which Chief Justice Warren and his colleagues faced in 1954—are segregated schools inherently unequal? We face other questions as well: Is integration even feasible? Is it desirable?

I believe there are clear answers to each of these three questions:

> One, segregated schools *are* for the most part unequal today and likely to remain so for generations to come;
>
> Two, integration is feasible but only with a new and unprecedented national commitment to achieve integrated neighborhoods and improved economic opportunities for blacks;
>
> Three, integration is desirable—morally and practically. Morally for reasons which ought to be self-evident to any enlightened human being, and practically if our nation is not to break apart.

However, while the answers to the questions may be clear—at least to some—the means of bringing them into reality are complicated. At times they seem overwhelming. But no lofty goal was ever achieved without tremendous obstacles and pain.

First of all, let me expand on answer one. Segregated schools are unequal because they are so often the result of poverty. There is no black Scarsdale High or Grosse Point High or Beverly Hills High. Most black schools are the result of segregated *and* poor neighborhoods. They are located in areas of high unemployment, high crime, drugs, immigration, teenage pregnancies, gangs and gang warfare, and the like. It is simply not possible to drop first-rate schools into such an environment. The environment is critical. A recent federal study demonstrated that poor children in schools with high concentrations of impoverished children were *twice* as likely to score *below* the national average as poor children in low-concentration schools (Traub, 1994: 44). Gary Orfield conducted a study in San Francisco in which he found that even after additional spending programs at local schools, low-income Hispanic students who transferred to middle-class white schools did better than those who stayed behind.

David Armor, a critic of court-ordered desegregation, offers the brilliant insight that "a good strategy for improving academic performance of students is to improve their socio-economic conditions." (I am reminded of a New Yorker cartoon showing a wealthy, well-dressed businessman looking down on a bum in the street and saying to him: "If you had any initiative you'd go out and inherit a department store.") In any event, it is impossible for inner-city schools to surmount all of the problems of urban decay and degeneration. The problems are almost limitless—disintegrating families, lack of nutrition, lack of hospitals and prenatal health care, high infant-mortality rates, crime, drugs, teenage sex, child abuse, and the list goes on. The problems are of third-world proportions. Yes, there are the occasional exceptions like Debbie Meier in East Harlem, but they are just that—exceptions. For most black children, there are few miracles; there are mostly the "savage inequalities" which Jonathan Kozol has so brilliantly exposed. What Orfield calls "the self-perpetuating cycle of racial isolation" is disastrous to children. It must be broken. How then?

Let us turn the clock back for a moment. According to renowned American historian Arthur Link, "From the German surrender in 1945 to March 1947, the American government and people had kept western Europe from near starvation and economic collapse by an outlay of some $11,000,000,000 in UNRRA aide, loans, credits, and assistance of various kinds." After this, the United States in its fear of communist expansion, launched the Marshall Plan for the economic recovery of Europe. Consequently, from April of 1948 to December of 1951, the United States government provided European countries with over $12,000,000,000 in assistance. Translated into 1995 dollars, that amounts to more than 100 billion dollars in aid. In Link's words, "the launching of the Marshall Plan meant that hereafter the destinies of the American people were inextricably intertwined with the destinies of free peoples who stood on the dangerous frontier between a world in chains and a world struggling for a new birth and freedom" (Link, 1956: 671, 674).

A Marshall Plan for Inner Cities

I propose that the American government acknowledge that henceforth the destinies of its own white peoples are inextricably intertwined with the destinies of black people. In short, I suggest that if the government was willing to prop up Europe after the devastation of World War II, then the government should be equally willing to rescue its own peoples from the devastation of inner city blight and isolation. I believe that we should consider a Marshall Plan for our inner cities.

Why should "we"[1] contemplate spending a massive sum on rebuilding much of black America? Because it is in every citizen's best interests individually and collectively, because it is simply the right thing to do, because the failure to take dramatic steps will guarantee that conditions will get worse and worse leading to further riots, perhaps revolution, and at the very least, increased violence and conflagration. "What happens to a dream deferred," Langston Hughes asked, "does it dry up like a raisin in the sun, or does it explode?"

I believe the latter is virtually inevitable. The L.A. riots of 1992 were but a prelude of what "we" can expect unless a massive effort is mounted, aimed at delivering a piece of the American dream to all American children—not just the white, the middle and upper classes, and the power structure.

What would a Marshall Plan set out to do and how would it be funded? It would set out to create jobs, to rebuild inner cities, to build libraries, recreational centers, hospitals, schools, colleges and trade schools, service centers, job training centers, and so on. Perhaps, for a time, it would utilize the National Guard and bring troops back from Europe to be relocated in gang- and drug-infested areas to provide safety for working men, women, and children who are trying to live decent and responsible lives. Furthermore, it would provide substantial funds to clean up, rebuild, renovate, and restore existing schools—which are often so disgusting as to be a national source of shame.

The problems of inner city schools and their surrounding environments are utterly intertwined. We cannot just plop money into a program here or there and expect to make an appreciable difference. We must wage an all-out campaign to treat causes as well as symptoms. The causes are poverty and neglect; the symptoms are all the social and educational ills above. We ought not kid ourselves. The problems will remain, and they will worsen unless and until we take dramatic action: a Marshall Plan for black America.

Postscript

Of course, poverty and all its concomitant ills are not the sole purview of black America. Poverty is rampant among whites, Hispanics, Asians, and Native Americans as well—and the national sin of poverty needs to be addressed with a resolve equal to the Marshall Plan for black America which I propose. I have simply focused, in this chapter, on the special problems of a group of people with a unique history and unique curse to overcome.

Note

1   Who is "we?" The 20 percent of citizens who vote? The disenfranchised who are too demoralized to vote? The one in five children who now live in poverty in the Unites States? The one in three black males who are in the prison process? The 1 percent who control 48 percent of the nation's wealth?

Chapter 15

Soiling Children in America

We blame the victims ever so much for their own homelessness, yet how can we blame our own children?

—Yvonne Vissing

It is a spiritually impoverished nation that permits infants and children to be the poorest Americans.

—Marian Wright Edelman

The task of this essay is to convey just how disgraceful conditions for children are in America today. I want the reader to consider seriously a horrible notion: as a nation, we are badly mistreating—in Jonathan Kozol's word, soiling—a whole generation of children. We—the adults, voters, citizens, middle and upper class beneficiaries of the blessings of America—are responsible for allowing these conditions to prevail.

The conditions are by now so widespread and so well-documented it is hard to plead ignorance. Whether one subscribes to a conspiracy theory of deliberate hostility and aggression (Chomsky, 1996: 33), or to a malign neglect theory, the results are the same: huge numbers of children live in Dickensian penury within the wealthiest nation in the world. Since the politicians allow this to continue, since the average voter is not called upon to provide reform (voters are called upon, however, to reduce benefits for children), and since children themselves have no power, few advocates, and no leadership—it then falls to those who should care the most to speak out—parents, teachers, and educators. But before suggesting ways of speaking out, I feel impelled to lay bare the host of problems we face, using both cold statistics and graphic anecdotes.

The Problems We Face

Perhaps the best place to begin is with the simple fact that in 1994, according to the Census Bureau, 21.8 percent of American children lived in poverty (*Los Angeles Times*, June 12, 1996: A22). One out of every five. And, according to a 1996 study of the National Center for Children at Columbia University, between 1979 and 1994, "the number of children living in poverty in the United States grew from 3.5 million to 6.1 million. . . . During that period, the rate of poverty for children under six also grew drastically—from 18 percent to 25 percent." One out of every four. Over half a million children are homeless. According to the *New York Times*, "The latest research indicates that poor children in the United States are poorer than the poor children in most other industrialized nations because the gap between rich and poor is particularly large in the United States and because welfare programs here are less generous than abroad." As the *New York Times* reported, an analysis of eighteen nations by the Luxembourg Income Study (a nonprofit group) revealed that the United States, while enjoying the second highest level of economic output per person, nevertheless ranked sixteenth in terms of the gap between affluent and poor children. "Only in Israel and Ireland are poor children worse off than poor American youths" (August 14, 1995: A7). What is to me most shocking is the degree to which the U.S. Congress and the public at large can shrug off these statistics and go about its daily business: Congress going about the business of dealing with child poverty by "providing" *budget cuts* for the wealthy; and the public at large by either not voting at all or by voting in favor of cutting welfare programs for children (almost 70 percent of those on welfare *are* children), and for cutting or neglecting funds for schools, hospitals, and inner-city life. The sad irony is that today's problems, ignored and denied, have a way of reappearing tomorrow in even worse manifestations and in ways which more directly harm those who could have made a difference yesterday.

The Manifestations of Child Poverty

How does child poverty manifest itself? High rates of infant mortality in low income areas. Poor nutrition. A disproportionate rate of pediatric AIDS. A high rate of suicide. Teen and even preteenage pregnancy. Illiteracy. And, perhaps worst of all, a general sense among hordes of children of despair and utter hopelessness. One could perhaps understand a sort of elitist, racist writing off of lazy, profligate, immoral, poor adults as being worthless beings; but how do we understand the rejection of a generation of children as if they were so much trash? The United States now ranks behind nineteen other nations in infant mortality, and almost 13 million children have no health insurance. Also, the United States has the third lowest immunization rate in the western hemisphere (*Santa Monica Outlook*, January 20, 1992). A black American child is less likely to be adequately immunized against polio than a child in Libya or Iraq. Clearly, one-fifth of America's children are living in Third World conditions—or worse.

Assault on Children

As if sheer poverty were not enough, the children of America are subjected to even more hideous assaults on their humanity. Consider, for example, four social issues in which children are major victims of sicknesses in our culture and country and against which there is little public outcry or political effort to protect them: guns, drugs, pornography, and media manipulation.

Guns

First, consider guns. One clear statistic tells the story: "Between 1979 and 1991, nearly 50,000 children were killed by firearms—a total equivalent to the number of American battle casualties in the Vietnam War" (Children's Defense Fund, 1994: 1–5). The Children's Defense Fund which offers this statistic buttresses it with further startling examples of how children are besieged in America:

... A gun takes the life of a child every two hours—the equivalent of a classroom full every two days.
... Homicide is now the third leading cause of death for elementary and middle school children (ages 5 to 14).
... A child growing up in America is fifteen times as likely to be killed by gunfire as a child growing up in Northern Ireland [a country at war].

And to these statistics, we may add three more facts:

... Between 1984 and 1990, the rate of firearm deaths among black males aged 15 to 19 increased by 300 percent; the increase among white males that age was 50 percent.

... A survey of 1,000 elementary and high-school students in Chicago found that more than 25 percent had witnessed a homicide, 40 percent had seen a shooting, and more than 33 percent had seen a stabbing.

... Teenagers in the U.S. are more than twice as likely to be victims of violent crime as adults.

Jonathan Kozol brings these statistics to life in his recent book, *Amazing Grace: The Lives of Children and the Conscience of a Nation*. Describing the Mott Haven district of the South Bronx in New York, Kozol writes that, "In 1991, 84 people, more than 50% of whom were 21 or younger were murdered in the precinct. . . . On Valentine's Day of 1993, three more children and three adults were shot dead. . . ." (Kozol, 1995: 5). Every day, in virtually every major newspaper in the country we read of another child killed by a handgun—innocent bystanders, victims of berserk parents, accidental killings, gang victims, it matters little the explanation; the reality is wholesale carnage of children and a nation unwilling to protect its young. The NRA, the gun and ammunition manufacturers, the various political groups are all hell-bent on preserving this "Constitutional right to bear arms," although any semirational human can see that handguns, rather than making anyone safe, have turned the United States into the world's leader in homicide—with children as a major victim.

Drugs

Profit clearly takes precedence over the rights of children—not only to life, but to life without rampant fear. The profiteering of the drug industry is yet another example of how children are victimized. Around every inner city or non–upper class district public school, we find the drug dealers preying upon the young to enlist them as users, distributors, and youthful participants in the profit nexus. The police know they are there. The local politicians and neighborhood residents know they are there. Still it continues. I have yet to hear a good explanation as to why we cannot keep school zones clear of drugs. Again, children are unable to defend themselves. Who will defend them?

Child Pornography

The profit motive has spawned yet another child-victimization industry—the child pornography business. The business ranges from the not terribly subtle advertising of the pouty-lipped, children-as–sex objects posing as models of clothes such as Guess Co. to the outright obscene use of children engaged in explicit acts. Child porn is now a multimillion dollar industry. A set of pictures of children (most often of girls) can fetch anywhere from one thousand to twenty thousand dollars (this includes the video market, and so on, where the advent of secret computer systems has made communication between pedophiles secure, international, and anonymous). At the upper end of the market, a child may actually be purchased as the customer's sex slave for a cost of between $50,000 and $200,000. Even in these tough economic times, this market is steadily growing.

Certainly we are looking at an international market as well. In cities such as Manila and Bangkok, the incidence of child prostitution is appalling. In Bangkok, for example, underage prostitutes range in the tens of thousands, while in Manila, "child prostitution rivals begging as the major occupation of the 50,000–75,000 street children who roam metropolitan Manila" (Campagna and Poffenberger, 1988: 147).

But one does not have to travel to the Far East to find such problems. They exist in America. It was estimated that in 1987, there were 1.3 million runaways in America and that about *half* of these were victims of some sort of commercial sexual exploitation (1988: 147). In America, "children are bought, sold, traded and misused in underground sex markets daily, and . . . the victims' immaturity make them vulnerable to entrepreneurs' manipulation" (1988: 4). As a nation, we will give headlines across the country to Lorena Bobbit or O.J. Simpson, but *not* to the daily abuse of children by quiet profiteers. The men involved in purchasing these favors must have large amounts of discretionary income. Hence, they're the rich, connected members of society—often pillars of the community, sometimes major contributors to major politicians. Consequently, few of them are ever brought to justice, and members of the Task Forces of both the Los Angeles Police Department and San Francisco Police Departmen are often unbelievably frustrated. They are allowed only to intercept a particular shipment, if they can; but are not able to pursue the cases any further up the chain. In other words, they hit the proverbial glass ceiling.

Experts in the field suggest that up to *1.5 million children* born outside the United States disappear into these markets each year. Some are routed into black market adoption rings. Some are sold into indentured slavery. But most are procured for some form of sexual exploitation. In the United States alone, the Department of Health and Human Services estimates that the number of children victimized by some form of commercial sexual exploitation (on a yearly basis) exceeds 1.2 million. Over half that number are subjected to "severe forms" of sexual exploitation. An undocumented child, smuggled into the United States as detailed in "EVIDENCE," has no records of birth, fingerprints, etc. Such children become the undocumented little Jane Doe's that turn up in dumpsters around big cities, leaving police few or no clues to pursue. The perpetrators simply move on to the next child.

Media Manipulation
Finally, children are targets of the media hucksters who see each child as a potential future buyer, as consumer clay ready to be shaped for a lifetime of junk consumption. In addition to the "normal" manipulation of the advertising industry, we find the purveyors of violence glorifying heroes with huge body counts to their credit, movies presenting human life as even cheaper than an already violent reality. It may be that establishing a direct link from television and film violence to violence in society is impossible to prove, but common sense would lead one to conclude that glorifying murder while making guns easily available to all citizens has had a major impact on making America the homicide capital of the world and placing American children among its leading victims.

The huge and overriding issue, the issue which threatens not only the future well-being of children in America in every respect, but the issue which subsumes so many other issues, the issue which tears at the very soul of the nation can be summed up in a single word: POVERTY. As we have seen in previous chapters, educational, social, cultural, economic, and political problems are inseparable. We truly do soil our children in America. We provide—for many—hideous living conditions, poor schooling, inadequate health services, dangerous neighborhoods, and disintegrating family structures. Yet, these are not separate problems: they are cut from a single cloth. Because it is a single ragged fabric, it is difficult to restore or repair it. We cannot simply pull out one damaged thread; the entire fabric needs attention.

Long-Term Consequences of Poverty

Jill Duerr Berrick, in her excellent study of women and children on welfare, *Faces of Poverty*, lists eight forms of poverty's violence against children, some she proclaims having "sad and irreversible consequences":

- Poor children are more likely to be born in poor health, to die in the first year of life, and to show signs of poor nutrition or malnutrition.
- Poor infants are less likely to have received prenatal care and are more likely to be born before term or at low birth weight.
- The rates of lead poisoning of poor children are so high that an estimated three million may be at risk of impaired mental and physical development.
- Poor children suffer higher rates of child abuse and neglect; they also are more likely to suffer from accidental injury or death.
- Poor children are more likely to have trouble in school, to repeat one or more grades, to have significantly lower IQ's, and to drop out as adolescents.
- Teen parenthood is most often found among young girls who were raised in poverty.

- Long-term poverty has long-term consequences. The longer household poverty lasts, the more likely children's home environments will deteriorate.
- Poverty begets poverty. Children raised in poor families are more likely to live in poverty or on the margins of poverty as adults, thereby repeating the cycle of disadvantage for their children (Berrick, 1995: 19–20).

So, while we may design programs to attend to this or that subset of the problem, the ultimate, overriding problem is poverty itself. What should be done?

The common sense answer, of course, is to decide—as the richest nation in the world—that poverty is unacceptable and then to make its eradication the *highest* priority in our national agenda. Is this likely to happen? Apparently not in Washington, D.C. or in the corporate board rooms. Where then might such a movement begin? I would argue that it must begin in the schools. Where else are children to look for advocates? Should not teachers be fierce and unrelenting in their protests against the tarnishing and trashing of children? The sad reality, however, is that teachers are all too often passive, hence tacit, defenders of the status quo. Many come together only under their union banners and only to fight for wages and benefits for themselves. Were they to fight equally hard for improving the conditions of poor children in this country, they would have a profound impact. Of course, if we paid teachers salaries commensurate with their value to society, they might be better able to defend children.

Specific Solutions for Poverty

Wendy Lazarus, co-founder and co-director of the Children's Partnership, affirms, "I think one of the most important lessons we've learned over the years is to be very specific about the problem and very specific about the solution" (Lazarus interview, 1994). She is right. Of course, this presupposes that we—as a nation—truly wish to find solutions. Making that assumption, I would like to offer the following solutions:

- Expand and fully fund Head Start centers across the country—make Head Start compulsory at age 4.

- Restore the arts (with trained artists and arts teachers) to inner-city schools, pre-school, family and day-care centers, boys and girls clubs, church youth groups, and company day-care programs.
- Reduce and strictly regulate the possession of handguns.
- Reduce the amount of violence on television and in films.
- Provide for a dramatic increase in the domestic peace corps: (a) to work for maintaining peace in neighborhoods; (b) to conduct intensive programs in parenting; (c) to create a peace-officer corps. This final suggestion was made by Geoffrey Canada:

> Peace officers would not be police; they would not carry guns and would not be charged with making arrests. Instead they would be local men and women hired to work with children in their own neighborhoods. They would try to settle "beefs" and mediate disputes. They would not be the eyes and ears of the regular police force. Their job would be to try to get these young people jobs, to get them back into school, and, most importantly, to be at the emergency rooms and funerals where young people come together to grieve and plot revenge, in order to keep them from killing one another (Canada, 1995: 60).

- Wage a *real* and comprehensive war on drugs in areas surrounding schools.
- Launch a massive effort to improve schools in poor districts: (a) cut class size in half; (b) rebuild collapsing, dilapidated schools; (c) build new state-of-the-art schools and classrooms; (d) hire first-rate teachers at honorable, attractive salaries.

Of course, there is far more we could do once we have decided as a nation that we want to truly keep the promises of the American dream for our children. For example, corporate America could organize itself to adopt schools—not just token P.R. campaign adoptions as is common today, and not to provide commercial (and hence, quasi-ideological) messages as, for example, Chris Whittle proposed to do with his "Channel One, Advertising in the Classrooms" proposals—but comprehensive, educational adoptions in which one corporation would assume responsibility for the education of the children in that school: curriculum programs, teacher training, purchase of state-of-the-art technology and textbooks, arts programs, and the like. Since corporations enjoy the legal status of a person, then why not *act* as compassionate "persons" and be a force for the rebuilding of America? In addition, I would suggest a national children's crusade in which parents, teachers, and children would organize a march to their local city halls and state capitals to call for cleaning up our schools and cities to make them decent places for children to learn and live within.

Additional Reforms

Finally, I would suggest a second Marshall Plan (see chapter 14) to create a safe, healthy America for our children. This plan would call for all the reforms listed above, as well as others, such as:

Creation of Children's Academies for Achievement (CAA)

The degree of abuse, neglect, relegation to poverty, and essential hopelessness, to say nothing of murder and trauma to which the children of America are subjected, is a national scandal and disgrace. Be they black, Asian, Hispanic, or white, children born into poverty are virtually doomed. Even bright, motivated, and talented children have the deck so stacked against them that only the "miracle-children" escape and succeed. There is little prospect at present that we will clean up, renovate, and revitalize the ghettoes of America. But we can remove children from them. A new nonprofit corporation—Children's Academies for Achievement—proposes to do just that: to establish public residential schools for disadvantaged urban and rural children. While this will not "save" all such children, it will rescue some. The basic idea is to provide children with a nurturing community, coupled with high academic programs. Their plan is to draw children from what is called the tenacious middle—children from severely disadvantaged backgrounds who nonetheless have continued to value and cling to the promise of school success. They are proposing to receive state support and to begin as charter schools. From my own experience, I can predict with a high degree of confidence that children attending such schools will break the cycle of hopelessness. They will be much less likely to drop out, join gangs, join the prison process; much less likely to join the ranks of the permanently *un*employable. A great deal of research back up this claim (Schuh and Canada, 1995). The investment in such schools and programs is cost effective by every standard imaginable.

Creation of Local Children's Authorities

One of the quiet tragedies occurring in America today is the disarray in services for abused and neglected children. Much of the material for the Children's Authority idea that follows is drawn from Lela B. Costin, Howard Jacob Karger, and David Stoeszela in *The Politics Of Child Abuse In America* (1996). "Plagued by underfunding and related problems—staff burnout, high turnover rates, large caseloads, poor working conditions, inadequately trained staff, and haphazard screening and investigative procedures," they say, "child protection has devolved into a virtual nonsystem." Of eight major industrial nations, the United States ranks the highest in child homicide and had more reports of child abuse in 1992 than all other industrialized nations (Italy, U.K., France, Japan, Canada, Germany, and Australia) *combined*. This is a shocking statistic. The creation of a single agency would eliminate "a tangle of overlapping services" and would make accountability and coordination easier to achieve. It would, in effect, "add a coherence of form and function that is absent in child abuse policy today" (Costin, Karger, Stoeszela, 1996: 171, 173, 176).

What Costin et al. propose is the creation of a single board of directors, similar to a school board, with elected officials who would appoint an executive director, who in turn would appoint heads of each of six divisions. This single agency would incorporate six major functions: (1) family support, (2) prevention/education services, (3) child placement [perhaps sending some children to Children's Academies For Achievement], (4) investigation, (5) enforcement, and (6) research and development (Costin, Karger, Stoeszela, 1996: 173 ff). The funding would come from a variety of public sources clearly outlined and thought out by the authors.

The authors of *The Politics Of Child Abuse In America* leave us with a haunting question: "After more than a century of efforts to protect abused children, have we the will to forge an adequate arrangement of programs for all American children?" They conclude, rightly, "The refusal to answer that question amounts to our failure to save the lives of innocent children" (Costin, Karger, Stoeszela, 1996: 187).

Focused Creation of Jobs in Areas with Fewer Intact Families

The strength and health of children are to a large degree dependent upon the strength and health of the family. The decline of intact families, and especially the absence of fathers in single parent families, can be traced largely to economic factors. Men who cannot find work suffer such a devastating loss of manhood that they often leave the home. The impact upon children is profoundly negative. We can break this cycle only by a massive plan to restore hope and opportunity for America's poor—a conscious, focused effort to create work in all of the slums and declining neighborhoods of the United States.

Earvin (Magic) Johnson took a significant leadership step in the inner city of Los Angeles recently with the development of the Magic Johnson Theatre Complex, which not only created new jobs, but provides neighborhood film entertainment. But we need projects like this to be launched all across the nation.

Everyone says education is the answer. But, if the education we provide poor children is inferior, then it is no answer at all. Thus, we are back to the same problem: most answers will cost large sums of money. We have the resources to acquire and spend this money. In 1948, we helped to rebuild Europe. In 1969, we put a man on the moon. What we lack is the will to get the funding from where it is. Where is it? It is in defense funding. It is in bureaucratic waste. It is in low sales taxes, gasoline taxes, and luxury taxes. It is in the top 20 percent of American families and corporations. Much of it is shielded, protected, and made unavailable to solve our national problems by a system of maximum profiteering and by the paid security guards of the rich—the three branches of government. The solution: teachers, parents, administrators, educators, and citizens of America—unite.

Chapter 16

Funding Solutions: Part I

For what shall it profit a man, if he
shall gain the whole world
and lose his own soul?

—The Gospel of St. Mark, 8:36.

By now, the overall theme of this book should be clear: our schools, our nation's children, and our futures are in deep crisis; this crisis is a reflection of political, social, and economic injustices, inequalities, and dysfunctions; and one cannot be solved without solving the others. While not all our problems are a function of money, many are. We cannot restore equity and decency to our schools and cities by simply streamlining bureaucracy (a favorite thought-deadening shibboleth), nor by eliminating administrative waste (another conventional notion). There simply is not enough "waste-money" in the systems.

The fact is that our schools and our cities are collapsing and we must design a drastic reordering of priorities and spending policies to rescue them. Anything short of this will resemble the cliché of rearranging deck chairs on the *Titanic*. A dramatic response is required to meet extreme crises. I would argue that *our nation's children should be our highest priority*—rather than the protection and preservation of wealth for the few whose fortunes are already at an outlandish *and rising* level. Furthermore, I believe we can no longer tiptoe around this issue, nor can we afford to allow the corporation servants in the press to avoid or discredit the issue by knee-jerk attacks on "liberalism" every time someone (be they conservative or liberal) tries to raise the issue. It is a matter of fairness: 20 percent of America's children are living in abject poverty while one percent of American families control 48 percent of America's wealth and wallow in luxury (Leone, 1995: vi). Either we acknowledge the disparity of wealth in this country and do something drastic about it, or we can look to a future in which we will surely have more frequent race riots, a more rapid deterioration of cities and small farms, an increased throwing on the ash heap of another generation of children (through pediatric AIDS, homicide, suicide, drugs, misery, homelessness, permanent unemployment, and so on), and a gradual erosion of the national soul. The pity and the unforgivable tragedy of it all is that it is correctable. We have the resources; we need to find the will to act. What would such actions involve?

Reallocation of Resources

The first step is to reset our national priorities and to agree that the education and welfare of our children along with the preservation of our national—and planetary—environment must be our overriding national goals. Once we accept this, we will need to decide how much of our annual national resources—our gross domestic product (GDP)—we are willing to spend on these goals. We might begin by examining what other countries spend on education and social welfare, and compare this to our own spending. For example, most European countries spend approximately 30 to 33 percent of their annual GDP on social welfare programs while the United States of America spends only 16 to 17 percent. Meanwhile, we spend a far higher proportion of our GDP on defense. Why? Against whom are we defending ourselves? Or are we only defending the privileges of the military industrial complex at the expense of our nation's future? Not for a minute would I argue that America should not have a strong, flexible, mobile armed forces to preserve peace in the world and at home, but surely we do not need to keep spending at World War II levels. "Without its military white corpuscles, the body politic will be defenseless before outside enemies. But if the military white corpuscles begin devouring the red corpuscles of the civil economy, the body politic will sicken and wither" (Calleo, 1992: 54). Surely we can now—finally—pay attention to our deteriorating social and physical conditions at home and reallocate our spending.

It is now time, in fact, long past time, for a shift from "defense" spending to spending on rebuilding America. For the fiscal year of 1996, Congress approved a defense budget of $243 billion while, for the same time period, it cut the National Endowment for the Arts budget 40 percent. This defense budget kept every controversial big ticket weapons project alive (stealth bombers and the like) at a cost of about $6.7 billion more than the administration requested. Yet we have the heartlessness to allow 20 percent of our nation's children to live in miserable poverty. Can there be any confusion about the values of the military-industrial-corporate oligarchies of the nation? If so, note that a recent study by the U.S. Nuclear Weapons Cost Study Project, a private group, has determined that *the U.S. has spent $3.9 trillion on nuclear weapons since 1945.* Is there any doubt who owns Congress? Rather than tamper with the industrialists' immense profits, Congress instead is willing to make socially irresponsible reductions in the safety net for poor people and the medical-security system for the elderly. It would be laughable if it were not, unfortunately, true.

It is one of the absolute wonders of the past seven years that the American public has so quickly forgotten and surrendered the anticipated benefits of the ending of the Cold War. The supposed peace dividends—that is, a transferring of funds to long neglected civic and social crises—has simply not happened. Military spending remains disproportionately high, the press is relatively silent about the matter, the public—easily led and misled—is not called upon to protest or to act, either by the press or their "leaders" in government, and the military-industrial profiteers continue to reap war-economy profits in a time of peace. It is absurd. Look for a moment at the price we (the vast majority of Americans) pay so that they (the military-industrial folks) can benefit (Melman, 1992: 1–17):

THEY "NEED":	WE FORFEIT:
$114 billion for 650 F-22 fighter planes	Modernization and expansion of all United States mass-transit systems
$100 billion for Trident II submarine and F-18 jet fighter programs	Cleaning up the 3,000 worst hazardous U.S. waste dumps
$25 billion for a fleet of C-17 jet cargo planes	Rehabilitation for more than one-million public housing units

THEY "NEED":	WE FORFEIT:
4.9 billion for the Atacm and Hellfire missile programs	Funding to allow all eligible children to enter the Head Start program
3.7 billion for the TOW-2 missile program	Medicare for an additional 4 million adults and 2 million children
2 billion for a single B-2 bomber	400 new elementary schools
1.4 billion for one Trident submarine	Global 5-year child immunization program against 6 diseases
479 million for 28 F-16 fighter aircraft	40,000 new teachers for United States schools

And the trade-offs go on and on. It is a matter of priorities. "Defense" we now know is clearly a euphemism for a *federal corporate/military/industrial welfare state*. The public is taxed and the government makes gargantuan grants to industrialists to build useless weapons, weapons which add nothing to the growth or welfare of the nation but a great deal to the wealth of a few. It is all a shrewd system which is concealed from the public—"a means to transfer money from the Treasury to the various defense industries, which in turn pays for the elections of Congress and President." It is little short of astounding how our nation has been able to maintain "defense" spending while effectively ignoring societal cesspools. Somehow the citizens of this country have been lulled into a drowsy acceptance of the notion "that we must ignore growing inequality and exclude from consideration tax policy options that attempt to ameliorate the situation" (Vidal, 1992: 31).

Reduce the National Debt by Eliminating the Grossest Features of the Corporate Welfare State

The reduction of interest payments on the national debt could make possible improving schools, rebuilding streets and highways, restoring safety to neighborhoods, placing uninsured citizens in medical plans, and so on. Legislators and economists know how to do this; they are, at present, afraid even to suggest reforming the corporate welfare system for fear of losing corporate support and, hence, losing elections. So, in addition to reducing the national debt, we must also institute campaign reform so that those to whom we look for reform are not *owned* by those in need of reform. It is clearly a major impasse we face, but if somehow we can find the leadership and the courage, we can change a system which is now clearly dysfunctional and cruel. But, let us set campaign reform aside for the moment and look at the corporate welfare state.

Many analysts have proposed a number of ways to reduce unfair corporate tax breaks and subsidies. As Daniel Franklin puts it: "Those waxing Smithian [as in Adam Smith] about getting government off business's back by deregulation are unabashedly granting industry enormous handouts in the form of tax breaks and subsidies that make aid to families with dependent children and subsidized school lunches look like a quarter in a coffee cup." Franklin adds that these subsidies "not only strain the budget (and thus put a squeeze on social spending) but . . . falsely prop up certain companies and industries, inhibiting beloved free competition" (1995: 670). Franklin lists ten such subsidies including: tax breaks for raids on workers pension funds, ethanol subsidy ($700 million), sugar subsidy ($1.4 billion), tax breaks for companies in U.S. territories ($3.5 billion), cash payments overseas to buy American weapons ($3 billion a year), special deductions for oil companies ($1 billion +), and FCC license giveaways (tens of billions).

Even *The People's Budget*—a conservative publication enthusiastically endorsed by Speaker Newt Gingrich—acknowledges that "you can find some form of corporate welfare tucked away in just about every corner of the federal budget" (Dale, 1995: 74–77). In addition to agreeing with Franklin about unnecessary tax breaks to oil and gas companies, *The People's Budget* comes up with its own list of unnecessary subsidies and tax breaks to corporations. What is most important is that these conservative authors who argue for downsizing welfare at least acknowledge that we also need to look at corporate welfare. The generous gifts which the government is providing the corporate and business sector are staggering and amount to a reverse welfare state—welfare for the already profitable *and* at the expense of the poor and suffering. What is staggering is not only the degree of this largesse, but the almost complete absence of scrutiny or demand for reform. In fact, as the gap between rich and poor is widening, the government's response is to reduce welfare for poor children.

But what of the argument that increased taxation will retard investment and hence restrict the creation of new jobs? I don't buy the argument. Companies with record earnings do not necessarily create new jobs; in fact, they often lay off workers in order to: (a) maximize profits for the few at the top; and (b) reach new record levels. On August 7, 1997, the Dow Jones Index reached the astounding level of 8,259. Were new jobs created? Was a single person removed from what we have now shamelessly classified as "the permanently unemployable"? No. Record earnings, maximum profits do not lead automatically to new companies, new ventures, and new employees. If this were really our concern, we could give tax credits to those who use their profits to create new jobs.

Even a cursory glance at corporate welfare will reveal funds needed to rebuild America without harming business. We are not talking about eliminating profits, but simply about reducing excessive profits to a more reasonable level. We are talking about providing our nation's children with a decent future.

Direct Taxation of Wealth

Edward N. Wolff, a noted economist and author, has written a clear and provocative study of the increasing inequality of wealth in America, entitled *Top Heavy*. This study, published by the Twentieth Century Fund Press, calls attention to some rather startling *facts*:

- during the 1980s *the top 1 percent* of wealth holders enjoyed two-thirds (66+ percent) of all increases in financial wealth;
- the bottom *80 percent* of households ended up with *less* real financial wealth in 1989 than in 1983;
- the median wealth of non-white citizens actually fell during the 1980s;
- the richest 1 percent of households own *48 percent* of America's wealth.

As Wolff summarizes, "the increase in wealth inequality recorded over the 1983–90 period in the United States is almost unprecedented. The only other period in the twentieth century during which the concentration of household wealth rose comparably was from 1922 to 1929. Then inequality was buoyed primarily by the excessive increase in stock values, which eventually crashed in 1929, leading to the Great Depression of the 1930s" (Leone, 1955: vi).

Given these discrepancies and given the dire conditions of schools and cities, a partial remedy would seem to suggest itself: the implementation of a modest wealth tax. Such a tax—as is the norm in Switzerland and France—with rates ranging from three-tenths of 1 percent (and an exclusion of about $50,000 in wealth) would have raised about $45 billion in 1994 or 1995. And, as Wolff points out: "In light of the recent monumental efforts to close the federal budget deficit by $50 billion, such a tax would go a long way toward achieving fiscal probity. Moreover, in the process, only 3 percent of families would have seen their federal tax bill rise by more than 10 percent" (Wolfe, 1995: 13).

I will backtrack a moment and clarify Wolff's distinctions between wealth and income: "Wealth refers to the net dollar value of the stock of assets less liabilities (or debt) held by a household at one point in time. Income, in contrast, refers to a flow of dollars over a period of time, usually a year" (1995: 41). Wolff, and others, are not proposing a new income tax (though they do not oppose a progressive income tax); rather they are proposing a very slight tax on the increase of wealth. Besides the obvious values of being equitable and generating badly needed revenue, there are two other arguments in favor of a direct tax on wealth. One, income is not by itself a completely accurate gauge of someone's well-being or capacity to pay taxes. Wealth is a better indicator. And two, an annual wealth tax "may induce individuals to transfer their assets from low-yielding investments to high-yielding ones." Finally, Wolff argues, there is no evidence (particularly when we look at foreign countries which *do* impose direct wealth taxes) that this tax would inhibit savings or that it would precipitate capital flight.

In 1994, 48,000 people lived in poverty in the South Bronx in New York. Their combined income was only $200 million. In that same year alone, one man made $1.1 billion. Something is wrong with this picture.

Reform Estate Tax Collection

The *New York Times* reported on December 22, 1996 that, "with maneuvers to bypass federal estate tax and possible under-reporting, one economist estimates, three-fifths of the wealthiest individuals' net worth at death is never taxed by the government" (Drew and Johnston, 1996: A1). So, while the government in the late 1990s seeks to "balance the budget" by cutting welfare payments for the poor, the wealthiest individuals and companies are devising new and more effective strategies of avoiding paying taxes which were never meant to level wealth, but simply to level the playing field. There are five such strategies which I believe warrant reevaluation and serious reform:

- The amount allowed to give or leave to one's heirs has been frozen at $600,000 for over a decade. during that time, the number of households which fall above that threshold has increased dramatically. In addition, as this book goes to press, Congress is discussing reintroducing a bill which the President vetoed in 1996 that would *raise* the tax-free exemption from $600,000 to $750,000! This plan is being aided by a lobbying coalition of business headed by former Senator Bob Packwood (Drew and Johnston, 1996: A14).
- Stock options have become a way for executives to amass great fortunes. But now these executives have devised a new way to avoid taxes: give these stock options away to one's children and grandchildren, which enables the giver to pay taxes on what the stock is worth today rather then what it might be worth tomorrow.
- There is yet a new method of avoiding inheritance taxes, a plan that gained popularity in the 1990s: parents transfer ownership of their homes to their children, live there rent free, and when they die, the house simply stays with the children without any estate tax.

· A fourth method of avoiding estate taxes is yet another new maneuver which is gaining popularity. This method allows people who own family corporations "to turn over a piece of these enterprises to their heirs while valuing those stakes at a discount" (Drew and Johnston, 1996: A15). Sometimes these discounts amount to 35 to 40 percent of their real values. The IRS had previously allowed discounts for non-family members on the theory that a buyer of the company would be buying incomplete control. But when the shares are held by family members, that argument is less valid. Yet the IRS has been unable to head this practice off in court cases.

· The fifth method of avoiding estate—as well as all other forms of income tax—is simply to underreport. With the number of cuts in IRS staffing (9 percent in 1995 and 1996), the percentage of estate tax returns that are audited has been dropping significantly since 1989. Furthermore, when the IRS challenges wealthy individuals, it is often simply outgunned in the legal maneuverings. How much income the federal government loses is anybody's speculation. No one, however, would argue that the amount is small.

What these five and other practices of estate tax avoidance add up to is a reduction of tax income of massive proportions. According to the *New York Times*, "What is most striking . . . is what could happen in coming years. The nation stands on the cusp of the largest transfer of wealth in its history, the $5 trillion to $10 trillion in assets that belong to the generations preceding the baby boomers. A significant share of that wealth could pass untaxed, some economists note, if the estate tax remains so easily circumvented" (Drew and Johnston, 1996: A14). Why is this a problem? Texas Representative Bill Archer, chairman of the House Ways and Means Committee, obviously does not see it as a problem. In fact, he boldly asserts—apparently feeling he has issued a generally accepted truism—"I want to get away from taxes that are meant to create some sort of social redistribution of wealth" (quoted in Drew and Johnston, 1996: A15). However, I believe this is exactly what taxes should do: create a redistribution of opportunity, to lift children out of penury, homelessness, and hopeless deprivation, to restore some sort of democracy to a country well on its way to becoming an unrepentant oligarchy.

Tax Shifts to be Levied upon
Activities Harmful to Society

David C. Korten, author of a disturbing new book, *When Corporations Rule the World*, suggests a new principle of tax policies: taxes, he writes, "should be assessed against those activities that contribute to social and environmental dysfunction. Therefore, corporate tax laws should be revised to shift taxes from things that benefit society, such as employment—including employer contributions to Social Security, health care, worker's compensation—in favor of taxing activities that contribute to social and environmental dysfunction, such as resource extraction, packaging, pollution, imports, corporate lobbying, and advertising" (Korten, 1995: 315). To Korten's list I would add alcohol, tobacco, gasoline, and guns and ammunition. Such taxes would cut down on the use of products which harm society profoundly in terms of medical costs (from alcoholism, lung cancer, air pollution related diseases). Of course, such taxes would also increase revenue. Our society would benefit at both ends. As Korten explains:

> Such taxes would cascade up through the system and discourage the use of socially and environmentally harmful products. For example, a tax at the source on coal, oil, gas, and nuclear energy would increase end-user prices and encourage conservation and conversion to solar energy sources, such as solar heating, wind, hydro, photovoltaic, and biomass. Resulting increases in transportation costs would provide a nondiscriminatory natural tariff to encourage the localization of markets. The added cost of automobile commuting would encourage investment and public transit and locating closer to one's work. A tax on pollution emissions would encourage pollution control. A tax on the extraction of virgin materials would encourage conversion to less polluting, less materials-intensive product designs and modes of production and a greater reliance on recycled materials. Assessing manufacturers an amount sufficient to cover estimated disposal costs of their product packaging would discourage unnecessary packaging. Import tariffs would support a strong self-reliant economy (Korten, 1996: 315).

As for guns and ammunition, besides making America the homicide capital of the world, and a ludicrous wild west show to the rest of humanity, gun victims are a major drain on our medical establishments. Like tobacco and alcohol, guns are a socially detrimental (to say the least) commodity. A severe tax on weapons and ammunition would serve two functions: one, to raise revenue for socially constructive, life-giving services; and, two, to reduce the costs of treating gunshot victims. As an extra benefit, if such a tax were to reduce the number of guns and ammunition purchased, then perhaps we might cut down on the wholesale carnage inflicted on children in this country. The question before us on this issue is, do we raise taxes on guns and ammunition in order to save lives, save medical costs, generate revenue to improve schools and cities, or do we allow the NRA and the gun profiteers to continue as they are?

To convey this message to the American public is, of course, a huge problem, and for one simple reason—the corporations own the media; they manufacture apparent consent with their agenda (Chomsky, 1988), and they eliminate any debate over policies which contribute to maximum profit. "The corporate grip on opinion in the United States is one of the wonders of the Western World. No First World [democratic] country has ever managed to eliminate so entirely from its media all objectivity—much less dissent" (Vidal, 1992: 41). Consequently, the public is never encouraged to think along lines of reforming the corporate welfare system, the American oligarchy, the corporate tyranny of America, and increasingly, the planet. It is a depressing scenario, but it is not irreversible. When the public finally realizes that its interests and its children's futures are being trampled by unbridled profiteering, then perhaps we will bring the economy back to the service of people. Teachers, one would hope, would have the wisdom and the courage to put forth this message.

Progressive Income Tax

One of the most dramatic and, I would argue, disgusting developments of the past decade and a half has been the growth of bloated salaries for the well-to-do. For example, in 1994, Louis V. Gerstner of IBM made a reported $12.5 million; Hugh McColl of National Bank earned $13.7 million; Alex Trotman of Ford took home $8.1 million. Yet while they were receiving such salaries, stock options, and other benefits, and as "their companies' earnings were booming, and as the gap between their pay and those of the average worker widened further . . . [they] were laying off hundreds of thousands of employees" (Shrag, 1995: A6). Look at the trend in the U.S.: "The 1960 after-tax average pay for CEOs was 12 times that of the average worker. By 1974, it was 35 times. In 1995, it was 135 times" (Meadows, 1995: M5). Much to the detriment of the national coffers, while CEOs and others at the top were enjoying elephantiasis of the salary, the national debt was rising and the phony (so called "tough") tax law of 1986 enabled the blessed at the top to pay even less than before. As Barlett and Steele report (1992: 7):

> Passage of the "toughest minimum tax ever" resulted in a 75 percent drop in the number of people who paid the tax, and a 90 percent drop in the amount they paid. On average, a millionaire in 1986 paid an alternative minimum tax of $116,395. Three years later, the average millionaire paid $54,758. *That amounted to a 53 percent tax cut* (emphasis added).

Did this mean that those at the top were paying more taxes at the regular rate and, hence, were not subject to the stricter alternative minimum tax? For some, this was true, but for millionaires and other upper income folks, it was not.

> From 1986 to 1989, the average tax bill of millionaires—exclusive of the alternative minimum tax—fell 27 percent, dropping from $864,068 to $634,196. At the regular tax rates, that represented a tax savings of $229,873 (Barlett and Steel, 1992: 7).

I would argue that a pure progressive income tax, fair, without loopholes, is a legitimate, ethical, and logical way to find funds for America's future. In terms of what is fair, Derek Bok (1993: 275) explains: "In some respects, the progressive tax is the ideal way to remove excessive earnings in a highly imperfect market. Because the Internal Revenue Service already exists, higher taxes for the wealthy will require little or no added administrative burden. Moreover, unlike remedies tailored to specific professions, progressive tax rates apply to all higher income and, hence, do not run the risk of driving talented people arbitrarily from one occupation to another."

On the subject of a progressive income tax, there is one more thought to consider. Milton Friedman, among others, argues that this tax "seems a clear-cut case of using coercion to take from some to give to others and thus to conflict head-on with individual freedom" (quoted in Bok, 1992: 276–77). Here I would argue that the higher value is the greatest good of all people as opposed to the greatest acquisitiveness of the few. Derek Bok properly responds to Friedman's argument by asserting that Friedman "overlooks the possibility that limiting the freedom of the well-to-do may be outweighed by expanding the freedom of the less fortunate" (Bok, 1992: 277). This is a choice we ought to make.

Chapter 17

Funding Solutions: Part II

Never doubt that a small group of thoughtful committed citizens can change the world. Indeed, it's the only thing that ever has.
—Margaret Mead

Once we accept the rather modest principles that we ought to preserve the planet, to provide for the poor, and to promote the well-being of the entire populace and not just the top 4 percent of the economic ladder, then a host of resources becomes available. The trick at present is to break through an unacknowledged wall of silence. As we saw in chapter 9, the oligarchies have succeeded in convincing the majority of the nation that they do not exist. The media, of course, are their loyal partners in this charade. Consider for a moment the resources that become available, however, once one accepts the principles of preservation of the planet, elimination of poverty, and well-being of all citizens. Donald L. Barlett and James B. Steele offer many suggestions in their 1992 study *America: What Went Wrong?* Here are but ten:

- Draft legislation that would encourage the creation of jobs that actually pay middle-class wages—rather than rewarding short-term investments that lead to the elimination of jobs.
- Reward corporations for investing in research and development which would lead to new jobs over the long-term—rather than actually penalizing companies for making such investments, as the current tax code inadvertently does.
- Develop legislation to assure that residents of foreign countries who invest in the U.S. pay income taxes on those

earnings at the same rates paid by U.S. residents with comparable incomes.

- End tax subsidies for companies that eliminate jobs in the U.S. and create jobs offshore.
- Enact legislation that would repeal the virtually unlimited deduction for interest on corporate debt.
- Reduce the tax deduction granted to banks for bad loans.
- Put an end to a system that allows members of congress and other public employees to draw larger pensions than their final salaries.
- End the various deductions and practices which allow profit-making companies and wealthy individuals to pay taxes at a lower rate than middle-class families.
- End the payment of social security benefits to the wealthiest recipients.
- Enact new laws to reward state and local governments that establish progressive tax structures (Barlett and Steele, 1992: 217–218).

The authors conclude their book with a response to the book which was published in the *Philadelphia Inquirer*. It bears repeating:

> To the extent that federal policy, rather than impersonal economic factors, is responsible for the hardships our citizens are suffering, there is reason to hope for the better . . . *we* make those policies through our elected representatives. What we make, we can unmake."

Make Corporations Pay More of Their Share of Taxes

There is yet another *way* to fund our future—"our" referring to the 96 percent not at the top, to the 20 percent of American children living in poverty, to the declining middle class, and to the vast number of citizens who enjoy fewer and fewer of the benefits of the country as the 4 percent appropriate more and more. The way is to restore equity to the balance between what corporations pay in taxes and what individuals pay. During the most recent gilded age (the 1980s), the burden has shifted from the corporations and landed on the backs of individual taxpayers. The following chart, derived from the Internal Revenue Service figures, tells the tale (Barlett and Steele, 1992: 47).

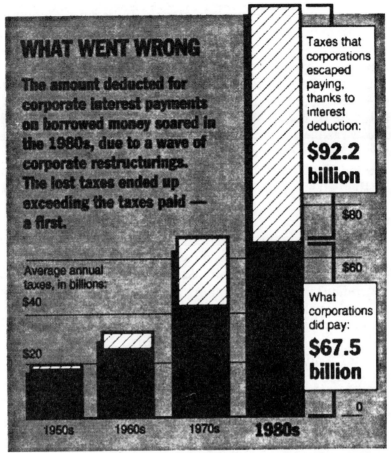

WHAT WENT WRONG

The amount deducted for corporate interest payments on borrowed money soared in the 1980s, due to a wave of corporate restructurings. The lost taxes ended up exceeding the taxes paid — a first.

Taxes that corporations escaped paying, thanks to interest deduction:

$92.2 billion

$80

Average annual taxes, in billions:

$40

$60

What corporations did pay:

$67.5 billion

$20

0

1950s 1960s 1970s **1980s**

SOURCES: Internal Revenue Service, Bureau of Economic Analysis

Just returning to the policies of the 1950s would restore billions to federal revenues and would enable us to attend to the disgraceful conditions so prevalent today in American schools and cities.

Design New Ways to Measure the Real Economy

Finally, I suggest that we design and implement new ways of measuring the health of the economy. Currently, the GDP is an index which we all blindly accept without challenge. In fact, the GDP is an arbitrary and recent invention based upon a principle which I believe is ultimately self-destructive—the principle of maximizing economic growth. To be sure, growth is a bewitching principle. Yet, taken to the maximum, it can only lead to the destruction of the human race as we know it, along with untold numbers of other species.

In January of 1972, *Ecologist Magazine* published a special issue called "A Blueprint for Survival" in which it declared that, "the principal defect of the industrial way of life with its ethos of expansion is that it is not sustainable" (Goldsmith et. al., 1972: 2). In the same year, the Club of Rome commissioned a study, "The Limits to Growth," which concluded that we have less than 100 years in which our profligate raping of the planet can continue and that "a decision to do nothing is to increase the risk of collapse" (quoted in Anderson, 1991: 4). As Dr. E.F. Schumacher pointed out in his classic study, *Small Is Beautiful*, economic growth promotes "an attitude toward life which seeks fulfillment in the single-minded pursuit of wealth. . . . [It is inadequate] because it contains within itself no limiting principle, while the environment in which it is placed is strictly limited" (quoted in Anderson, 1991: 5). The GDP is thus the evaluative tool of our own destruction.

Victor Anderson and many others have suggested alternative economic indicators to measure the human and physical health of a nation's economy. Anderson, for example, suggests three parallel ways of considering the economy:

1 the economy considered from a monetary or financial point of view [as we now do];
2 the economy considered as consisting of human beings organized together in particular ways; and,
3 the economy considered as a set of arrangements for mediating the relationship between human beings and the natural world (Anderson, 1991: 46).

Thus, if we take track 2 seriously, we would have to measure things such as indicators of work and unemployment, consumption of food and minimum daily caloric requirements per capita (as the world health organization calculates), indicators of health—i.e., infant mortality rate (IMR), and a host of social indicators: i.e., net primary school enrollment, illiteracy rates, percentages of the population with access to health coverage, and the like. Then if we take track 3 seriously, we need to expand our measurements to include systems of environmental accounting. As Anderson explains, "these systems follow the same general pattern as company financial accounts" (1991: 65). For each resource, there are opening and closing accounts including such areas as tropical deforestation, extinction of species, the greenhouse effect, soil erosion, population, energy consumption, and the like.

Replacing the GDP with the GPI

The current GDP is oblivious to what Thomas Berry refers to as the "earth deficit." This more comprehensive approach to measuring/evaluating our economy has been given further support by a new organization called Redefining Progress, a nonprofit public policy organization in San Francisco. They propose replacing the GDP with a new measurement, the GPI— Genuine Progress Indicator. A recent article in *The Atlantic Monthly* explains why:

> By itself the GDP tells very little. Simply a measurement of total output, it assumes that everything produced is by definition "goods." [Thus] when the United States fishes its cod populations down to remnants, this appears on the national books as an economic boon— until the fisheries collapse. As the former World Bank economist, Herman Daly, puts it, the current national-accounting system treats the earth as a business in liquidation. (Cobb, Halstead, and Rowe, 1995: 65–66)

In addition to the "earth deficit," the Redefining Progress group points out the failure of the GDP to measure the social realm. Consequently,

> the GDP totally ignores the distribution of income, for example, so that enormous gains at the top—as were made during the 1980s—appear as new bounty for all. (Cobb et al., 1995: 67)

The proposed GPI suggests a whole series of new statistical resources we could use that would better measure our human and habitat gains and losses. A few factors they suggest are:

- The Household and Volunteer Economy—i.e., taking care of children and the elderly, cleaning and repairing, contributing to neighborhood groups.

- Crime—the GDP counts as *progress* the money people spend deterring crime. The GPI includes hospital bills and property losses arising from crime and the locks and electronic devices that people buy to prevent it.
- The Distribution of Income—measures the extent to which the *whole population* actually shares in any increase.
- Resource Depletion and Degradation of the Habitat—i.e., measures the using up of oil and other minerals as a cost of the national accounts.

Redefining Progress lists twenty such improvements. To implement such improvements will be enormously difficult—the current system favors those in power. The American citizens and a new generation of leaders must insist upon a fundamental principle: "What you increase isn't necessarily good"; that growth and economics generally must be a means to an end, and not an end in itself (Cobb et al., 1995: 78). If we were to revaluate *how* we measure our economy, we would begin to see things in a more rational manner and we would do our children and generations to come an incalculable service.

To summarize, there are dozens of resources available to our nation to build a better future. Capitalism itself is not the problem; it is, in fact, a potentially beneficial system. And socialism has not demonstrated a full understanding of the human psyche. The importance of personal initiative is not to be minimized; it is, in fact, an important ingredient in individual happiness and success. My concern is with unbridled capitalism. We simply need to control runaway profiteering. It will not wash to say, "The poor have always been with us," or to allow billionaires to say, "Taxes are killing me," or to neglect human and earth deficits. The lack of revenues *are* literally killing children and undermining the vitality of our country and our natural resources. The funds are there. Solutions are possible. Educators, citizens, and leaders with vision and integrity must regain the soul of our country. It must all, I believe, begin in the schools across the land.

Chapter 18

A Curriculum for the Soul

A person's life purpose is nothing more than to rediscover, through the detours of art, or love, or passionate work, those one or two images in the presence of which his heart first opened.

—Albert Camus

When we want to understand something we cannot just stand outside and observe it. We have to enter deeply into it and be one with it in order to really understand.

—Thich Nhat Hanh

Ultimately, the problem young people today have is making sense of their lives. It is, of course, the problem every human being confronts at some time or other. It is referred to by existentialists as the human condition or the human predicament. But it is a predicament which has been compounded and made seemingly insoluble in the twentieth century. Science has exploded many comforting myths; astronomers have demonstrated the infinitesimally puny place the earth occupies in the cosmos; psychology has split the human personality into many parts; physicists have shown the essentially indeterminate nature of matter and the relativity of time and space; world religions continue to foment disharmony and strife rather than harvest the fruits of community; anthropologists seem to demonstrate that god(s) are manmade; politicians too often prove to be corrupt, egoistic, even pathological; consumer-oriented cultures offer little more than vanity and the void; while traditional/indigenous cultures sink further into the mire of depression and hopelessness. It is a discouraging scene. Try as we may to anesthetize ourselves to it all through drugs, or consumption, or isolated self-centeredness, the hunger for meaning remains. It remains because what we "lovest well" continues to survive in our inner being despite the constant barrage of trivia and violence. We yearn for a sense of wholeness.

And schools? Do they address this yearning, this hunger? Rarely. Instead, they retreat to simplistic notions of "achievement" through test scores and Grade Point Average badges of merit, and, in so doing, simply ape the very culture which is starving the young. They are not beacons; they are mirrors. Those who seek to teach values all too often impose a kind of rigid fundamentalism upon their charges which will not stand up to the very real complexities of the late-twentieth and emerging twenty-first century and which, if they do not leave the young disillusioned and confused, run the risk of producing a new round of bigotry and exclusivity.

The Search for Meaning in Schools

The challenge for schools is to help the young find meaning in the world they live in; a world dominated by the codes of greed and progress no matter what the human and environmental cost, of racial and ethnic divisiveness, of widening separation between rich and poor, and of religious factionalism. These are matters of profound import which, if ignored, leave the young frightened and demoralized. How can a high school or college allow its graduates to move on if it has not addressed these matters and placed them at the center of the curriculum? If schools do not explore these questions in depth, then where will the young student, the adult, find a place to receive any kind of guidance, any help toward seeking some sort of light? I do not suggest that there are easy answers to the perplexities of life in the twentieth/twenty-first centuries. But asking and living with the questions is a major source of relief for the young. They feel that the adults they would like to trust are now simply practicing a monumental form of denial. They know irrelevance when they see it. They know that getting grades, that doing well on quizzes and tests, that getting into this or that college should not be the soul purpose of education or life. Yet, if this is all the adults preach, how can the young be anything but disillusioned? However, when adults allow them to ask their life questions, to discuss their fears and dreams, to consider things of the spirit, then they feel that their education has some integrity to it. The search for meaning is each student's unique journey, and somehow schools must find ways to help the young to take their inner journey and to do so in ways which connect with the greater community of human beings. It is a daunting task. Yet to neglect the task will surely render schools irrelevant, if not downright irresponsible.

The privilege, the gift, the opportunity that each of us has in our brief, extinguishable blink of time is so precious that what we do in the schools takes on cosmic significance. Each of us is a soul breathing the breath of the living universe. We inspire and are inspired by life. Education should be "learning the language of being alive." If this phrase of Charles Olson's resonates at all with readers of this book, then what schools should be becomes unbelievably exhilarating. If we have the courage and imagination to so conceive them, schools may be places where students would become fully alive—to inhale the life of the mind and spirit and to exhale joy and creativity. Is this possible? Of course. We have all had glimpses of such. We have had small or great epiphanies where a teacher, a poem, an insight quickened our very soul and where the mystery and majesty of life became apparent—in a waterbead, an image, a watercolor, a theorem. But how to structure such a curriculum; how to design a school dedicated to awaken the intelligence of the heart?

Actually, I have already outlined many such processes in previous chapters. But it is important to note that there are avenues by which schools—even the very best—work at cross-purposes. J.M. Krishnamurti writes that, "without leisure there can be no learning." Yet in most schools, there is little leisure. There is, instead, an endless round of classes, lectures, tests, term papers, and deadlines. There is little time for meandering down intriguing side paths where discoveries are often made. There is little opportunity for silence and meditation. Yet when, seemingly by accident, we do provide students with leisure and silence, they respond in ways they and we could never have imagined in conventional systems. Thus we face the dilemma of wanting to teach skills, impart knowledge, and engender concepts while creating systems of education which militate against the kind of inspired learning that ought to be the highest goal of education.

The dilemma is ultimately irresolvable. At best, there can only be a dynamic tension between the two forces, and within that tension there will be moments of balance or creative imbalance which provide the juice and the brightness of learning. What is crucial, however, is that the two forces are honored and given their due. All too often schools neglect the meditative, the leisurely, the silent, the poetic, the artistic, and students are left only with pressure, routine, and the prosaic. The two forces work in creative tandem only when each is respected by both student and school. But it is the school's responsibility to help the student experience and understand the dilemma itself.

The Spiritual Needs of Students

What I am suggesting here is that schools consciously acknowledge and attempt to honor a "curriculum for the soul," to explore what Wallace Stevens referred to as "the wild country of the soul." Students, in fact all people, have a hunger to discover meaning in life, to fill the void. Yet it seems as though our culture—and our schools as reflectors of that culture—virtually sponsors the void. Our schools put up metaphoric signs which say, "Do not feed the students: let them eat spiritual dust." But it *is* possible to feed the spiritual needs of students without violating the separation of church and state. We can begin by giving them a time and place to discuss matters of the spirit. Programs which provide a one-hour-a-week opportunity to discuss life's mysteries with a sympathetic adult lift students' spirits immensely. We can also provide them with role models in history and contemporary society to study. Heroes and sheroes are important to young people; they need people to admire. Yet schools—when they attend to this need at all—too often only bring on campus a football player or a rock star to speak to the children. And what do they model? Too often, simply immense wealth—the kind of wealth 99.8 percent of the students will have no possibility of attaining. There are other models available—social workers, founders of grassroots community organizations, campaign reform advocates, and so on, people whose careers are socially beneficial and whose jobs are attainable.

In addition, we can attend to the spiritual dimension by designing curricular topics of study which excite the imagination of young people. One afternoon, when I was seventeen years old, I remember absentmindedly pulling a book off a library shelf whose title intrigued me: *Where Angels Dared to Tread*. Written by B.F. Calverton and published in 1941, and it was a study of utopian communities in America. I was dumbfounded. I had never heard of such places. That people were willing to give up their normal lives to seek to build these remarkable places—Brook Farm, New Harmony, and so on—was exciting. Later in graduate school, I returned to the topic, comparing Bellamy's *Looking Backward*, Howells's *A Traveler From Altruria*, Thoreau's *Walden*, and B.F. Skinner's *Walden Two*. Being encouraged to imagine better ways of doing things excited me, and it excites young people. It gives them a sense of the possible. School, all too often, is a place which reconfirms what social conditions seem to mandate—that which is not possible! Thus the study of heroes and utopias is a valuable antidote to cynicism and despair.

Now, we may pause and ask, of what possible relevance are these reflections to an inner-city teacher with five to six classes a day of 30 to 40 students per class in a violence-torn, gang-infested, low-income, family-fragmented community? Perhaps the answer is "very little." But, of course, in such conditions few other suggestions of any kind are of much relevance. Very little learning can take place and very little does within the crazy chaos of poverty and ghettoization. But *if* we were to:

... clean up and rebuild neighborhoods;
... provide job opportunities to restore dignity to neighborhood dwellers;
... clean up and rebuild schools;
... cut class size in half;
... restore the arts to the curricula;
... include community service, human development, environmental studies and field trips in each student's course of study;
... pay teachers respectable wages,

then we could better address matters of the human spirit. In fact, if we did the above, the human spirit would begin to flourish quite naturally. Herding children and their families into inner-city concentration camps, i.e., urban reservations, is not only inhuman, it seems almost a deliberate policy designed to kill the human spirit of those who cannot afford to escape. But if we were to build into their neighborhood and their school day certain key ingredients for which the soul hungers, we would see less anger, less alienation, and less violence. What I am proposing is that public school children be provided with the same blessings as the top private schools in the country. At Crossroads School, as we have seen, these blessings are not *extra*curricular; they are graduation requirements. So what would a curriculum of the soul look like?

A Curriculum of the Soul

Time–for leisurely discoveries, day-dreaming,
    conversation;
Space–for quiet reflection, for safe places to walk, for
    listening to music;
Ceremony–to honor the human spirit;
Storytelling–to connect to one's roots, traditions,
    history; to connect to one's inner self;
Mysteries–to discuss life's deepest mysteries;
The Arts–to express one's uniqueness, one's vision of life;
Global/Cultural Studies–to learn and celebrate diversity;
Global Ecology–to learn of interdependence;
The Study of Heroes and Utopias–to stimulate the
    imagination.

None of these curricular suggestions are beyond our reach nor are they "radical" or "far out." They are not liberal or conservative. They are simply intelligent ways of dealing with terrible social and cultural conditions. We are a nation that has lost its way. Virtually every politician, social commentator, cultural critic bemoans our loss of values, the decline of religion, the gross and obscene excesses of the media, our children's lack of moral standards. Yet, educational reformers seem only to call for better test scores, more academic demands—as if this would address our deeper maladies and hungers. Ironically, our students' grades and test scores will improve once they see school as a meaningful place in their lives. Our national sickness is a sickness of the soul. This is the place where we need to seek remedies.

Chapter 19

Coda

There was a house made of dawn. It was made of pollen and of rain, and the land was very old and everlasting. There were many colors on the hills, and the plain was bright with different-colored clays and sands. Red and blue and spotted horses grazed in the plain, and there was a dark wilderness on the mountains beyond. The land was still and strong. It was beautiful and all around.

—N. Scott Momaday

Come, my friends
'Tis not too late to seek a newer world.

—Alfred, Lord Tennyson, "Ulysses"

At the beginning of this century, men in white jackets came around at night to light the gaslights in the streets. By 1972, we had landed twelve men on the moon. In 1946, the first IBM computer, on display at 57th Street and Madison Avenue in New York, was a monstrosity of a machine; now, tiny laptops can perform far greater computations, more rapidly. Technology, automation, computerization have not only advanced beyond anyone's wildest imaginings, but the advances continue at an accelerated pace. The last fifty years exceeded the previous thousand and the last ten exceeded the previous fifty. Where it all will lead ultimately is a matter of pure speculation, but certain immediate implications are clear and ought to guide educators, parents, and political and civic leaders as they plan for the coming decades and century.

The Myths of Technology

There are certain mythic balloons which we must quickly puncture. Technology does not automatically lead to more job opportunities. How this delusion has been promulgated is just short of astounding. How and why people have bought it is equally puzzling. In fact, technology frequently eliminates more jobs than it creates. The example of big automated farms driving small farmers off the land into big cities—where many become and remain unemployed—is but one example. Consequently, one reads of big corporations firing (the current euphemisms are "corporate restructuring" or "downsizing") large numbers of employees. Of course, as long as the profit factor is the primary guiding principle of the economy, then more and more workers will be fired without regard for the human havoc such massive firings wreak. "Labor-saving devices" often end up being "labor destroying devices." Global unemployment is at its highest point since the Great Depression of the 1930s. More than 800 million people are now unemployed or underemployed in the world (Rifkin, 1995: xv). "Labor-saving devices" truly are "profit-saving devices" whose benefits accrue primarily to the elite but rarely to the workers. The fact is that we have millions of people unemployed, and more people working longer hours for less pay and declining benefits.

As if this were not unfair enough, the rapid acceleration of technology/communications/automation/etcetera has a second dire consequence: it widens the already huge chasm between the rich and the poor. Refined and increasingly sophisticated means of advancement and the opportunities to succeed become available to a smaller and smaller elite group as educational opportunities and access to the complex technocommunications industry become more and more a function of being wealthy. As Paul Kennedy explains in his sobering study, *Preparing for the Twenty-First Century*, "Today's global financial and communications revolution is also more intense than in that earlier era [a generation ago]." Kennedy affirms that, "whereas many individuals and firms seem well positioned for the twenty-first century, relatively few nations appear to be" (1993: 332, 334). Clearly in the United States, while certain individuals and firms are well positioned, a large majority of the middle class and almost all of the lower class, the underclass, and the homeless and "permanently unemployable" are simply excluded entirely from playing the game.

We must, however, try to remember that technological advances and discoveries need not be economic ends in themselves. They can be means to human ends. Thus far, we have tended to apply their benefits almost exclusively to profit-and-loss statements rather than to systems of well-being for human beings. But this could change if we *first* considered priorities, *then* implemented technology according to those priorities. Unfortunately, "human beings are usually unwilling to make short-term sacrifices to achieve a distant improvement in the general good—and most politicians' perspectives are shorter still" (Kennedy, 1992: 336). As Jeremy Rifkin writes: "The wholesale substitution of machines for workers is going to force every nation to rethink the role of human beings in the process. Redefining opportunities and responsibilities for millions of people in a society absent of mass formal employment is likely to be the single most pressing social issue of the coming century" (1995, xv).

A Shift in Priorities

What might such a future look like? If we were to dramatically shift our priorities, how would education change? What would our schools or society come to value and to implement? For one, we would make a commitment—as a nation—to a fully employed citizenry. This would be accomplished by providing a guaranteed job and, hence, a guaranteed income for all individuals and households. We might, for example, calculate job hours to provide the services needed to administer, renovate, rebuild, and refurbish the country, divide those hours by the work force, and pay everyone a living wage, even if the hours were fewer than eight-a-day.

Rifkin proposed another variant of this approach by suggesting that we direct what he calls the third sector (also known as the independent or volunteer sector) to a serious and substantial rebuilding of America. He suggests that the government provide incentives to encourage those who do have jobs but are working fewer hours to work in community service areas, and to employ millions of permanently unemployed Americans in neighborhood and infrastructure jobs. Rifkin suggests tax deductions for community-service hours and "social wages" for work rather than unemployment payments. He also proposes a guaranteed annual income. He concludes his study with the statement that, "the end of work could spell a death sentence for civilization as we have come to know it. The end of work could also signal the beginning of a great social transformation, a rebirth of the human spirit. The future lies in our hands" (Rifkin, 1995, 293).

Once everyone has a job, a roof overhead, and adequate medical coverage, then we can pay more attention to quality-of-life issues. How will schools prepare people not just for vocations, but for living? What will people do with their increased hours not at work? The answer is both simple and complex. They will *live*. They will pursue hobbies, passions, avocations they have always wanted to pursue. They will seek to develop their talents—be they meager or major. For example, I enjoy writing poetry; I have no illusions of being the next James Merrill, but I do value the poems I write when I have occasional quiet moments. The work gives me a sense of accomplishment and satisfaction. This discovery of poetry came to me from school. This is what schools can do for all of us—open doors, provide a bibliography for the rest of one's life, to teach life-skills, to show children what is possible. Schools of the future will not be just places to learn how to climb up the economic ladder, but instead they will be places where students—of all ages—learn the arts of living: these arts would include play (everything from chess to playing a musical instrument); the arts themselves—music, dance, theatre, visual arts, creative writing, storytelling; written history and oral histories; gardening and crafts; filmmaking and photography—the list is virtually endless. Many of these classes are now available in some schools and colleges, but in the new society I am proposing, the priorities in people's lives would shift dramatically from vocation to avocation, from the pressure of *getting* a job and *making* a living to deriving satisfaction *in living*.

The possibilities for schools and for society are immense. As the coming of a new century fires the imaginations of people from all corners of the globe, one can only hope that Americans will look closely at what need not be, and resolve to bring about what should and what ought to be. So we come full circle: as I maintained in the preface to this book, the problems of

American schools are a function of the problems of society, and we cannot solve the former without solving the latter.

Good News and Bad News

The good news is that the problems of both are not unsolvable. One source for optimism is that many problems are a consequence of limited consciousness; as consciousness expands, our ability to see problems more accurately and to design more effective reforms expands simultaneously. Our knowledge of the environmental threat has grown considerably. If we can raise an awareness of our interdependence with the natural world into an even higher level of consciousness, then our progress on the environmental front will grow exponentially. Similarly, our awareness that growth is not an end in itself is beginning to come into wider circles of discussion. If we can help our children see that human values transcend profit margins, then perhaps we can slow down the devastation inflicted upon human beings and the environment by mindless "growthism." Also, our awareness of significant and substantive gender issues has come into wider consciousness during the past few decades. That consciousness has then led to the implementation of meaningful changes and reforms for women.

We are, however, lagging in our perception of the national tragedies of poverty, the neglect and degradation of children, the full extent of the two Americas—black and white, the disgraceful conditions which prevail in public schools across the land, and the discrepancies between what we preach about democracy and what we practice. What we fail to see and to teach in our schools is that these problems, these social tragedies, these national dysfunctions are all interrelated and drag us all down. They ruin the lives not only of the have-nots, but they threaten the well-being of all—*including the haves.* In some places, the very wealthy have built virtual fortresses protected by armed guards to isolate themselves from the rest of humanity whom they fear. But, ultimately, a society filled with angry, alienated, ill-educated, unskilled, and unemployable young people will not only lead to increased violence and economic calamities, but such a society will lessen the joy and possibilities of all who live within its boundaries.

A Premise that Could Transform America

I would like to conclude by stating a premise that, if taken seriously by every citizen and by every educator, would, I believe, transform America and, given America's immense wealth and world leadership, would help transform the world. It is a simple premise, but its implications are huge. It is a moral and ethical premise as well; it is, in fact, at the heart of our Declaration of Independence and Constitution. We have just not yet made it the priority that governs our societal behavior and national and educational policies. It is also at the heart of Jesus' teachings and the teachings of other worldwide religious figures. The premise is this:

> *That the lives of children born everywhere are of inherently equal value, and that providing all children with equal opportunities for health, education, and a decent life ought to be the highest priority of all individuals, institutions, and nations.*

Who could disagree with this? Still, it is not what consciously motivates our social structure, nor our economy, nor our government's behavior both at home and abroad, nor, in many cases does this premise motivate our schools' curricula and classroom teachings. But it is not too late. Not yet.

Reference List

1. The Goals of Education: What Is Truly Basic?

Lewis, C.S. 1947. *The Abolition of Man*. New York: Macmillan.

Schweitzer, Albert. 1933. *Out of My Life and Thought*. New York: Henry Holt.

Whitehead, Alfred North. 1929. *The Aims of Education*. New York: Macmillan.

2. Anger and Alienation: What to Do About It

Gardner, Howard. 1993. *Multiple Intelligences; The Theory in Practice: A Reader*. New York: Basic Books.

————. 1983. *Frames of Mind: The Theory of Multiple Intelligences*. New York: Basic Books.

3. The Power of the Arts

Cleveland, William. 1994. "Why the Visual Arts Must Be in the School Curriculum." *The College Board Review* (Fall, No. 173).

Lehrer, Leonard. 1994. "Why the Visual Arts Must Be in the School Curriculum." *The College Board Review* (Fall, No. 173).

Rockefeller Panel Report. 1965. *The Performing Arts: Problems and Prospects*. New York: McGraw-Hill.

U.S. News and World Report. 1992 (March 30).

Venerable, Grant. 1988. *The Paradox of the Silicon Savior*. Richmond, CA: Ventek.

4. Mysteries: Educating for Hope and Community

Crossroads School. 1990. *The Mysteries Sourcebook: A Teacher's Guide*. Santa Monica, CA: Crossroads School.

Faulkner, William. 1967. *The Portable Faulkner*, ed. Malcolm Cowley. New York: The Viking Press.

Kessler, Shelley. 1990. "The Mysteries Program: Educating Adolescents for Today's World." *Holistic Review* (Winter).

Seal, Kathy. 1993. "At the Crossroads: A Unique Public/Private School Coalition." *Spirit* (Pacific Southwest Airlines magazine) (September): 80–82.

Zimmerman, Jack, and Virginia Coyle. 1996. *The Way of Council*. Las Vegas: Bramble Books.

5. The New Social Studies, Part I: Global Issues

Kennedy, Paul. 1993. *Preparing for the Twenty-first Century*. New York: Random House.

Weber, Peter. 1994. *Net Loss: Fish, Jobs, and the Marine Environment*. Worldwatch Paper 120: July.

6. The New Social Studies, Part II: American Issues

Allen, Paula Gunn, Lee Francis, Linda Hogan, Simon Ortiz, Carter Revard, Ray A. Young Bear. 1991. *Columbus and Beyond*. Tucson, Arizona: Southwest Parks and Monuments Association.

Chomsky, Noam. 1993. *The Prosperous Few and the Restless Many*. Berkeley: Odian Press.

Kozol, Jonathan. 1975, 1990. *The Night Is Dark and I Am Far from Home*. New York: Simon and Schuster.

Phillips, Kevin. 1991. *The Politics of Rich and Poor*. New York: Harper Perennial.

Takaki, Ronald. 1994. "Reflections in a Different Mirror." *Teaching Tolerance* (Spring): 15.

7. A New Cosmology: Honoring the Blue Planet

Berry, Thomas. 1988. *The Dream of the Earth*. San Francisco: Sierra Club Books.

Deloria, Vine Jr. 1994. *God Is Red*. Golden, CO: Fulcrum Publishing.

Jeffers, Robinson. 1987. *Rock and Hawk*, ed. Robert Hass. New York: Random House.

McGillis, Sister Miriam. 1990. *Fate of the Earth* (audio tape). Available from Genesis Farms, Blairstown, New Jersey 07825.

Sawyer, Kathy. 1995. "Universal Truths." *The Washington Post National Weekly Edition* (September 11–17): 6.

8. Advancing to Less

Abbey, Edward. 1988. *One Life at a Time, Please*. [especially the chapter "Arizona: How Big Is Big Enough?"] New York: Henry Holt.

Berry, Wendell. 1990. *What Are People For?* San Francisco: North Point Press.

Brown, Lester R., Christopher Flavin, Sandra Postel. 1991. *Saving the Planet*. New York: W.W. Norton.

Greenberg, Jonathan, and William Kistler. 1992. *Buying America Back*. Tulsa, OK: Council Oak Books.

Raskin, Marcus, and Chester Hartman. 1988. *Winning America: Ideas and Leadership for the 1990s*. Boston: South End Press.

Roszak, Theodore. 1973. *Where the Wasteland Ends*. New York: Anchor Books.

9. Who Will Tell the Children?

Chomsky, Noam. 1992. *What Uncle Sam Really Wants*. Berkeley: Odonian Press.

Forster, E.M. 1938. "What I Believe." *Two Cheers for Democracy.* New York: Harcourt.

Lewis, Charles. 1996. *The Buying of the President.* New York: Avon Books.

Lind, Michael. 1995. "To Have and Have Not." *Harper's* (June): 36.

Parenti, Michael. 1995. "Popular Sovereignty vs. The State." *Monthly Review* (March): 6.

Vidal, Gore. 1992. "Monotheism and Its Discontents." *The Nation* (July 13): 56.

Wills, Gary. 1996. "Hating Hillary." *The New York Review of Books* (November 14): 13.

10. Crossroads: A Carnival That Works

Crossroads School

A collection of newspaper and magazine articles, brochures, and video tapes are available from the Office of Community Relations, Michele Hickey, Director, Crossroads School, 1714 21st Street, Santa Monica, CA 90404, (310) 829-7391.

12. The Quest for Unity: One Language, Many Stories

Schlesinger, Arthur M., Jr. 1992. *The Disuniting of America: Reflections on a Multicultural Society.* New York: W.W. Norton.

Stannard, David E. 1992. *American Holocaust: Columbus and the Conquest of the New World.* New York: Oxford University Press.

Zinn, Howard. 1992. *Columbus, the Indians, and Human Progress:* 1492–1992. Westfield, NJ: Open Magazine Pamphlet Series.

13. Gender Studies: She, He, and We

Women's Studies

American Association of University Women. 1992. *How Schools Shortchange Girls.* New York: Marlowe.

Baym, Nina. 1992. *The Feminism and American Literary History.* Brunswick, NJ: Rutgers University Press.

Orenstein, Peggy. 1994. *Schoolgirls: Young Women, Self-Esteem, and the Confidence Gap.* New York: Anchor Books.

Sadker, Myra & David. 1994. *Failing at Fairness: How America's Schools Cheat Girls.* New York: Macmillan.

———. 1985. "Sexism in the Schoolroom of the '80s." *Psychology Today* (March): 19.

14. A Marshall Plan for Black America

Hacker, Andrew. 1995. *Two Nations: Black and White, Separate, Hostile, Unequal.* New York: Charles Scribner's Sons.

Orfield, Gary. "Ghettoization and Its Alternatives," in Paul E. Peterson, ed. *The New Urban Reality.* Washington, DC: Brookings Institution: 161–196.

———, Susan Eaton. 1996. *Dismantling Desegregation.* New York: New Press.

15. Soiling Children in America

Berrick, Jill Duerr. 1995. *Faces of Poverty: Portraits of Women and Children on Welfare.* New York: Oxford University Press.

Campagna, Daniel S., and Donald L. Poffenberger. 1988. *The Sexual Trafficking in Children.* Dover, MA: Auburn House Publishing.

Canada, Geoffrey. 1995. "Peace in the Streets." *Utne Reader* (July–August).

Costin, Lela B., Howard Jacob Karger, and David Stoesz. 1996. *The Politics of Child Abuse in America.* New York: Oxford University Press.

Kozol, Jonathan. 1995. *Amazing Grace.* New York: Crown Books.

16 and 17. Funding Solutions: Parts I and II

Anderson, Victor. 1991. *Alternative Economic Indicators.* London: Routledge.

Barlett, Donald L., and James B. Steel. 1992. *America: What Went Wrong?* Kansas City, MO: Andrews and McMeel.

Bok, Derek. 1993. *The Cost of Talent: How Executives and Professionals Are Paid and How It Affects America.* New York: Free Press.

Calleo, David P. 1992. *The Bankrupting of America.* New York: New York University Press.

Franklin, Daniel. 1995. "Ten Not So Little Piggies." *The Nation* (November 27).

Korten, David C. *When Corporations Rule the World.* West Hartford, CT: Kumarian Press, 1995; and San Francisco: Beckett-Koehler Publishers; 1995.

Melman, Seymour. 1992. *Rebuilding America: A New Economic Plan for the 1990s.* Westfield, NJ: Open Magazine Pamphlet Series.

Vidal, Gore. 1992. *The Decline and Fall of the American Empire.* Berkeley, CA: Odonian Press.

Wolff, Edward N. 1995. *Top Heavy: A Study of the Increasing Inequality of Wealth in America.* New York: Twentieth Century Fund Press.

19. Coda

Kennedy, Paul. 1993. *Preparing for the Twenty-first Century.* New York: Random House.

Rifkin, Jeremy. 1995. *The End of Work.* New York: A Jeremy P. Tarcher/Putnam Book.

Further Reading

1. The Ends of Education: What Is Truly Basic?

Berry, Wendell. 1990. *What Are People For?* San Francisco: North Point Press.

Cummins, Paul. 1992. *Dachau Song: The Twentieth-Century Odyssey of Herbert Zipper.* New York: Peter Lang Publishing.

————. 1971. *Richard Wilbur: A Critical Essay.* Grand Rapids, MI: Eerdmans Publisher.

Dewey, John. 1967. *Dewey on Education*, ed. Martin S. Dwerkin. Columbia, New York: Teachers College Press.

Forster, E.M. 1951. "What I Believe," in *Two Cheers for Democracy.* New York: Harcourt, Brace and World.

Freire, Paulo. 1990. *Pedagogy of the Oppressed.* New York: Continuum Publishing.

Gardner, Howard. 1983. *Frames of Mind: The Theory of Multiple Intelligences.* New York: Basic Books.

Hutchins, Robert M. 1953. *The Conflict of Education: In a Democratic Society.* New York: Harper and Brothers.

Peters, R.S., ed. 1973. *The Philosophy of Education.* London: Oxford University Press.

Postman, Neil. 1995. *The End of Education.* New York: Alfred A. Knopf.

Power, F. Clark, Ann Higgins, and Lawrence Kohlberg. 1989. *Lawrence Kohlberg's Approach to New Education.* New York: Columbia University Press.

Read, Herbert. 1943. *Education Through Art.* London: Faber & Faber.

2. Anger and Alienation: What to Do About It

Baca, Jimmy Santiago. 1992. *Working in the Dark: Reflections of a Poet of the Barrio*. Santa Fe, NM: Red Crane Books.

Davis, Mike. 1992. *L.A. Was Just the Beginning: Urban Revolt in the United States*. Westfield, NJ: Open Magazine Pamphlet Series.

Deloria, Vine Jr. 1988. *Custer Died for Your Sins*. Norman, OK: University of Oklahoma Press.

Fromm, Erich. 1955. *The Sane Society*. New York: Holt, Rinehart.

McCall, Nathan. 1994. *Makes Me Wanna Holler: A Young Black Man in America*. New York: Random House.

Rodriguez, Luis J. 1993. *Always Running: La Vida Loca: Gang Days in L.A.* New York: Simon and Schuster.

Rose, Mike. 1989. *Lives on the Boundary*. New York: Penguin Books.

Takaki, Ronald. 1994. *From Different Shores*. New York: Oxford University Press.

Wideman, John Edgar. 1984. *Brothers and Keepers*. New York: Holt, Rinehart and Winston.

3. The Power of the Arts

Dewey, John. 1934. *Art as Experience*. New York: Capricorn Books.

Gardner, Howard. 1989. *To Open Minds*. New York: Harper-Collins.

———. 1993. *Multiple Intelligences: The Theory in Practice*. New York: Basic Books.

Lindstrom, Miriam. 1957. *Children's Art*. Berkeley, CA: University of California Press.

Madeja, Stanley S., and Sheila Onuska. 1977. *Through the Arts to the Aesthetic*. St. Louis: Cemrel.

May, Rollo. 1975. *The Courage to Create*. New York: W.W. Norton.

Quinn, Thomas, and Cheryl Hanks. 1977. *Coming to Our Senses: The Significance of the Arts for American Education*. New York: McGraw-Hill.

Read, Herbert. 1966. *The Redemption of the Robot: My Encounter with Education Through Art*. New York: Simon and Schuster.

————. *The Meaning of Art*. 1931. Baltimore, MD: Penguin Books.

————. *Education Through Art*. 1943. London: Faber & Faber.

Zipper, Herbert. Various articles and speeches. See the bibliography in *Dachau Song*, by Paul Cummins.

4. Mysteries: Educating for Hope and Community

Castaneda, Carlos. 1981. *The Eagle's Gift*. New York: Pocket Books.

Gardner, Howard. 1993. *Multiple Intelligences: The Theory in Practice*. New York: Basic Books.

Goleman, Daniel. 1995. *Emotional Intelligence*. New York: Bantam Books.

Niehardt, John G. 1959. *Black Elk Speaks*. New York: Pocket Books.

Sparrow, Norbert. 1995. "The Children's Council." *LA Parent Magazine* (September): 54–55.

5. The New Social Studies, Part I: Global Issues

Asimov, Isaac, and Frank White. 1991. *The March of the Millennia*. New York: Walker.

Bello, Walden. 1994. *Dark Victory: The United States, Structural Adjustment and Global Poverty*. London: Pluto Press.

Brown, Lester R. 1995. *State of the World* [an annual publication, 1984–1997]. New York: W.W. Norton.

Chomsky, Noam. 1991. *The New World Order*. Westfield, NJ: Open Magazine Pamphlet Series.

———. 1992. "Year 501-World Orders, Old and New: Parts I & II." *Z Magazine* (August/July).

———. 1991. *Terrorizing the Neighborhood*. Stirling, Scotland: AK Press.

Michaelson, Karen L., ed. 1981. *And The Poor Get Children: Radical Perspectives on Population Dynamics*. New York: Monthly Review Press.

Roszak, Theodore. 1992. *The Voice of the Earth*. New York: Simon and Schuster.

6. The New Social Studies, Part II: American Issues

Caldicott, Helen. 1991. *Towards a Compassionate Society*. Westfield, NJ: Open Magazine Pamphlet Series.

Chomsky, Noam. 1992. *Chronicles of Dissent*. Monroe, ME: Common Courage Press.

———. 1991. *Deterring Democracy*. New York: Hill & Wang.

———. 1988. *Manufacturing Consent*. New York: Pantheon Books.

Croteau, David, and William Haynes. 1994. *By Invitation Only: How the Media Limit Political Debate*. Monroe, ME: Common Courage Press.

Frank, Robert H., and Philip J. Cook. 1995. *The Winner-Take-All Society*. New York: The Free Press.

Galbraith, John Kenneth. 1992. *The Culture of Contentment*. New York: Houghton Mifflin Co.

Holmes, Stephen. 1995. *Passions and Constraint: On the Theory of Liberal Democracy*. Chicago: University of Chicago Press.

Jorgen, Randolph, ed. 1992. *Columbus and Beyond*. Tucson, AZ: Southwest Parks and Monuments Association.

Kennedy, David M. 1995. "Savage Words, Deadly Deeds." *Los Angeles Times* (April 30).

Kraus, Mickey. 1992. *The End of Equality*. New York: Basic Books.

Lappé, Frances Moore. 1989. *Rediscovering American Values*. New York: Ballantine Books.

Lind, Michael. 1995. *The Next American Nation*. New York: The Free Press.

McCarthy, Eugene J. 1982. *Complexities and Contraries: Essays of Mild Discontent*. New York: Harcourt Brace Jokanovich.

Vidal, Gore. 1992. *The Decline and Fall of the American Empire*. Berkeley, CA: Odonian Press.

7. A New Cosmology: Honoring the Blue Planet

Berry, Wendell. 1970. *The Hidden Wound*. New York: Ballantine Books.

Bowers, C.A. 1993. *Education, Cultural Myths, and the Ecological Crisis*. Albany: State University of New York Press.

———. 1995. *Educating for an Ecologically Sustainable Culture*. Albany: State University of New York Press.

Brown, Lester R., Christopher Flavin, and Sandra Postel. 1991. *Saving the Planet*. New York: W.W. Norton.

Elgin, Duane. 1993. *Awakening Earth: Exploring the Evolution of Human Culture and Consciousness*. New York: William Morrow and Co.

Etzioni, Amitai. 1993. *The Spirit of Community: The Reinvention of American Society*. New York: Simon and Schuster.

Fox, Matthew. 1983. *Original Blessing*. Santa Fe, New Mexico: Bear & Co.

Gore, Al. 1992. *Earth in the Balance*. New York: Houghton Mifflin Co.

Levitt, Peter, trans. 1991. *Pablo Neruda Sky Stones*. Los Angeles: William Dailey.

Lovelock, J.E. 1979. *Gaia: A New Look at Life on Earth*. Oxford: Oxford University Press.

Meadows, Donnela, Dennis L. Meadows and Jorgen Randers. 1992. *Beyond the Limits*. Post Mills, VT: Chelsea Green Publishing Co.

Myers, Norman. 1990. *The Gaia Atlas of Future Worlds*. New York: Anchor Books.

Ornstein, Robert, and Paul Ehrlich. 1989. *New World, New Mind*. New York: Touchstone.

Robinson, J.A.T. 1963. *Honest to God*. Philadelphia: The Westminster Press.

Roszak, Theodore, ed. 1995. *Ecopsychology*. San Francisco: Sierra Club Books.

Schumacher, E.F. 1975. *Small Is Beautiful*. New York: Harper Perennial.

Stegner, Wallace. 1962. *Wolf Willow: A History, a Story, and a Memory of the Last Plains Frontier*. New York: Viking.

Teilhard, de Chardin. 1959. *The Phenomenon of Man*. New York: Harper.

Thoreau, Henry David. *Walden and Other Writings*. Numerous publishers.

Vitek, William, and Wes Jackson. 1996. *Rooted in the Land: Essays on Community and Place*. New Haven: Yale University Press.

Weber, Peter. 1994. "New Loss: Fish, Jobs, and the Environment." *The Worldwatch Institute*. Washington, D.C. (July).

8. Advancing To Less

Anderson, Victor. 1991. *Alternative Economic Indicators*. London and New York: Routledge.

Athanasiou, Tom. 1996. *Divided Planet: The Ecology of Rich and Poor*. Boston: Little Brown.

Brown, Lester R. 1996. *State of the World* [An Annual Publication, 1984–1997]. New York: W.W. Norton.

Durning, Alan. 1992. *How Much Is Enough? The Consumer Society and the Future of the Earth*. New York: W.W. Norton.

Goodman, Paul and Percival. 1947. *Communitas*. New York: Vintage Books.

Harrington, Michael. 1986. *The Next Left: The History of a Future*. New York: Henry Holt.

Keyes Jr., Ken. 1985. *The Hundredth Monkey*. Coos Bay, OR: Vision Books.

Krugman, Paul. 1994. *The Age of Diminished Expectations*. Cambridge, MA: MIT Press.

Lewis, C.S. 1947. *The Abolition of Man*. New York: Macmillan.

Mannes, Marya. 1958. *More in Anger*. New York: J.B. Lippincott.

Nisbet, Robert. 1988. *The Present Age: Progress and Anarchy in Modern America*. New York: Harper and Row.

9. Who Will Tell the Children?

Alexander, Herbert E., and Anthony Corrado. 1995. *Financing the 1992 Election*. New York: M.E. Sharpe.

Bok, Sissela. 1978. *Lying: Moral Choice in Public and Private Life*. New York: Pantheon Books.

Chomsky, Noam. 1994. *Secrets, Lies and Democracy*. Tucson, AZ: Odonian Press.

———. 1993. *The Prosperous Few and the Restless Many*. Berkeley, CA: Odonian Press.

Edsall, Thomas B. 1984. *The New Politics of Inequality*. New York: W.W. Norton.

Greider, William. 1992. *Who Will Tell the People?: The Betrayal of American Democracy*. New York: Simon & Schuster.

Horwitt, Sanford D. 1989. *Let Them Call Me Rebel: Saul Alinsky, His Life and Legacy*. New York: Knopf.

Kempton, Murray. 1992. "The Democratic Vista." *The Nation* (November 13): 49.

Lapham, Lewis H. 1988. *Money and Class in America*. New York: Weidenfeld and Nicholson.

Lasch, Christopher. 1995. *The Revolt of the Elites and the Betrayal of Democracy*. New York: W.W. Norton.

Phillips, Anne. 1993. *Democracy and Difference*. University Park, PA: Pennsylvania State University Press.

Phillips, Kevin. 1993. *Boiling Point*. New York: Random House.

Sussman, Barry. 1988. *What Americans Really Think: And Why Our Politicians Pay No Attention*. New York: Pantheon.

Wise, David. 1973. *The Politics of Lying*. New York: Random House.

Withers, Robert. 1995. Correspondence with Paul Cummins.

10. Crossroads: A Carnival That Works

Fliegel, Seymour, and James MacGuire. 1993. *Miracle in East Harlem*. New York: Random House.

Greenberg, Daniel. 1987. *Free at Last: The Sudbury Valley School*. Farmingham, MA: Sudbury Valley School Press.

Horenstein, Mary Ann. 1993. *Twelve Schools That Succeed*. Bloomington, IN: Phi Delta Kappa Educational Foundation.

Wood, George H. 1992. *Schools That Work*. New York: Penguin Books.

11. Independent Schools: Institutional Community Service

Bellah, Robert N., Richard Madsen, William M. Sullivan, Ann Swidler, and Steven M. Tipton. 1985, 1996. *Habits of the Heart: Individualism and Commitment in American Life*. Berkeley: University of California Press.

Camus, Albert. 1961. *Resistance, Rebellion, and Death*, trans. Justin O'Brien. New York: Alfred A. Knopf.

Coles, Robert. 1993. *The Call of Service: A Witness to Idealism.* New York: Houghton Mifflin.

Cummins, Paul F. 1992. *Dachau Song: The Twentieth Century Odyssey of Herbert Zipper.* New York: Peter Lang Publishing.

Cuomo, Mario. 1995. *Reason to Believe.* New York: Simon and Schuster.

Etzioni, Amitai. 1993. *The Spirit of Community: The Reinvention of American Society.* New York: Simon and Schuster.

Forché, Carolyn. 1981. *The Country Between Us* [Poetry]. New York: Harper and Row.

Goodwin, Richard N. 1992. *Promises to Keep: A Call for a New American Revolution.* New York: Times Books.

Harrington, Michael. 1962. *The Other America: Poverty in the United States.* New York: Macmillan.

Kozol, Jonathan. 1995. *Amazing Grace: The Lives of Children and the Conscience of a Nation.* New York: Crown Publishers.

Schweitzer, Albert. 1933. *Out of My Life and Thought.* New York: Henry Holt.

Stegner, Wallace. 1982. *One Way to Spell Man.* Garden City: Doubleday.

Wuthnow, Robert. 1991. *Acts of Compassion: Caring for Others and Helping Ourselves.* Princeton, NJ: Princeton University Press.

12. The Quest for Unity: One Language, Many Stories

Chavez, Linda. 1991. *Out of the Barrio: Toward a New Politics of Hispanic Assimilation.* New York: Basic Books.

Galbraith, John Kenneth. 1992. *The Culture of Contentment.* New York: Houghton Mifflin.

Galeano, Eduardo. 1993. *Walking Words.* trans. Mark Fried. New York: W.W. Norton.

Hughes, Robert. 1993. *Culture of Complaint: The Fraying of America*. New York: Oxford University Press.

Morgan, Edmund S. 1975. *American Slavery: American Freedom*. New York: W.W. Norton.

Shorris, Earl. 1995. *Latinos: A Biography of the People*. New York: W.W. Norton.

Simonson, Rick, and Scott Walker. 1988. *Multi-Cultural Literacy: Opening the American Mind*. St. Paul: Graywolf Press.

Takaki, Ronald. 1989. *Strangers from a Different Shore: A History of Asian Americans*. New York: Penguin Books.

———. 1993. *A Different Mirror: A History of Multicultural America*. Boston: Little Brown.

13. Gender Studies: She, He, and We

Women's Studies

Belenky, Clinchy, Goldberger and Tarule. 1991. *Women's Ways of Knowing*. New York, Harrington Park Press.

Brown, Lyn Midel, and Carol Gilligan. 1992. *Meeting at the Crossroads*. New York: Ballantine Books.

Freedman, Estelle. 1981. *Their Sisters' Keepers: Women's Prison Reform in America, 1830–1930*. Ann Arbor: University of Michigan Press.

———. 1996. *Maternal Justice: Miriam Van Waters and the Female Reform Tradition*. Chicago: University of Chicago Press.

Gabriel, Susan, and Isaiah Smithson. 1990. *Gender in the Classroom: Power and Pedagogy*. Chicago: University of Illinois Press.

Heilbrun, Carolyn E. 1988. *Writing a Woman's Life*. New York: Ballantine Books.

Human Rights Watch. 1995. *The Human Rights Watch Global Report on Women's Human Rights*. New York: Human Rights Watch.

Levitt, Ilene. *An Evaluation of an Intervention Program for Teachers to Improve Gender Equity in Classrooms.* Ph.D. dissertation #920–7622, Ann Arbor.

Maher, Francis A., and Mark Kay Tetreault. 1994. *The Feminist Classroom.* New York: Basic Books.

Mann, Judy. 1994. *The Difference: Growing Up Female in America.* New York: Warner Books.

Murdock, Maureen. 1990. *The Heroine's Journey.* Boston: Shambhala Publications.

Pipher, Mary. 1994. *Reviving Ophelia: Saving the Selves of Adolescent Girls.* New York: Ballantine Books.

Politt, Katha. 1995. *Reasonable Creatures: Essays on Women and Feminism.* New York: Vintage Books.

Richardson, Laurel, and Verta Taylor. 1993. *Feminist Frontiers III.* New York: McGraw-Hill.

Woods, Peter, and Martyn Hammersley, eds. 1993. *Gender and Ethnicity in Schools.* London: Routledge Press.

Men's Studies

Bly, Robert. 1990. *Iron John: A Book About Men.* New York: Addison-Wesley.

Campbell, Joseph. 1949. *The Hero with a Thousand Faces.* Princeton: Princeton University Press.

Ehrenreich, Barbara. 1993. *The Hearts of Men: American Dreams and the Flight From Commitment.* New York: Anchor Press/Doubleday.

Gerzon, Mark. 1983. *A Choice of Heroes.* Boston: Houghton-Mifflin.

Gilmore, David D. 1990. *Manhood in the Making: Cultural Concepts of Masculinity.* New Haven: Yale University Press.

Hawley, Richard A. 1996. *Boys Will Be Men: Masculinity in Troubled Times.* Middlebury, VT: Paul S. Eriksson Publisher.

Johnson, Robert A. 1977. *He: Understanding Male Psychology*. New York: Harper and Row.

Jung, Carl G. 1989. *Aspects of the Masculine*. Princeton, NJ: Bollingen Press.

Maas, James. 1985. *Speaking of Friends: The Variety of Man-to-Man Friendships*. Berkeley, CA: Shameless Hussy Press.

Osherman, Samuel. 1986. *Finding Our Fathers: The Unfinished Business of Manhood*. New York: The Free Press.

14. A Marshall Plan for Black America

Abernathy, Ralph David. 1989. *And the Walls Came Tumbling Down: An Autobiography*. New York: Harper Perennial.

Cone, James H. 1991. *Martin and Malcolm and America: A Dream or a Nightmare?* Maryknoll, NJ: Orbis Books.

Cose, Ellis. 1993. *The Rage of a Privileged Class*. New York: HarperCollins.

Duberman, Martin. 1964. *In White America*. New York: Signet Books.

Franklin, John Hope. 1976. *Racial Equality in America*. Chicago: University of Chicago Press.

Gates, Henry Louis, Jr. 1994. *Colored People*. New York: Alfred A. Knopf.

Kotlowitz, Alex. 1994. *There Are No Children Here*. New York: Random House.

Kozol, Jonathan. 1991. *Savage Inequalities: Children in America's Schools*. New York: Crown Publishers.

Link, Arthur S. 1956. *American Epoch*. New York: Alfred A. Knopf.

Massey, Douglas S., and Nancy A. Denton. 1993. *American Apartheid: Segregation and the Making of the Underclass*. Cambridge, MA: Harvard University Press.

Myrdal, Gunnar. 1944. *An American Dilemma: The Negro Problem and Modern Democracy.* New York: Harper and Bros.

Novick, Michael. 1995. *White Lies, White Power.* Monroe, ME: Common Courage Press.

Taverber, Kall. 1989. "Residence and Race: 1619–2019." In *Race: Twentieth Century Dilemmas–Twenty-First Century Prognoses.* Milwaukee, WI: University of Wisconsin (ed. Winston A. Van Horne): 229–251.

West, Cornel. 1994. *Race Matters.* New York: Random House.

Wilson, William J. 1987. *The Truly Disadvantaged: The Inner City, the Underclass, and Public Policy.* Chicago: The University of Chicago Press.

Zweigenhaft, Richard L., and William G. Domhoff. 1991. *Blacks in the White Establishment? A Study of Race and Class in America.* New Haven: Yale University Press.

15. Soiling Children in America

Blau, Joel. 1992. *The Visible Poor: Homelessness in the United States.* New York: Oxford University Press.

Boyer, Ernest. 1991. *Ready to Learn: A Mandate for the Nation.* Princeton, NJ: The Carnegie Foundation for the Advancement of Learning.

Cecil, Nancy Lee. 1995. *Raising Peaceful Children in a Violent World.* San Diego, CA: Luramedia.

Change, Hedy. 1993. *Affirming Children's Roots.* San Francisco: A California Tomorrow Publication (Fall).

Chomsky, Noam. 1996. *Class Warfare (Interviews with David Barsamian).* Monroe, ME: Common Courage Press.

Coles, Robert. 1986. *The Moral Life of Children.* Boston: Houghton Mifflin.

Edelman, Marian Wright. 1993. *The Measure of Success.* New York: Harper Perennial.

Galbraith, John Kenneth. 1993. *The Voice of the Poor*. Cambridge, MA: Harvard University Press.

Gans, Herbert. 1995. *The War against the Poor: The Underclass and Anti-Poverty Policy*. New York: Basic Books.

Goldscheider, Frances K., and Linda J. Waite. 1991. *New Families, No Families? The Transformation of the American Home*. Berkeley, CA: University of California Press.

Harrington, Michael. 1962. *The Other America: Poverty in the United States*. New York: MacMillan.

Hodgson, Lucia. 1997. *Raised in Captivity: Why Does America Fail Its Children?* St. Paul, MN: Graywolf Press.

Jencks, Christopher. 1994. *The Homeless*. Cambridge, MA: Harvard University Press.

Katz, Michael B. 1993. *The Underclass Debate: Views from History*. Princeton, NJ: Princeton University Press.

Kotlowitz, Alex. 1991. *There Are No Children Here*. New York: Doubleday.

Kozol, Jonathan. 1967. *Death at an Early Age*. New York: Penguin Press.

———. 1988. *Rachel and Her Children*. New York: Fawcett Columbine.

———. 1991. *Savage Inequalities*. New York: HarperCollins.

Lazarus, Wendy, and Laurie Lipper. 1994. *America's Children and the Information Superhighway*. Santa Monica, CA: Children's Partnership.

Lewis, Michael. 1978. *The Culture of Inequality*. Amherst, MA: University of Massachusetts Press.

———. 1995. *Improving Poor People: The Welfare State, the "Underclass," and Urban Schools as History*. Princeton, NJ: Princeton University Press.

Miller, Alice. 1983. *For Your Own Good: Hidden Cruelty in Child-Rearing and the Roots of Violence*. Hildegarde and Hunter Mannum. trans. New York: Noonday Press.

Polakow, Valerie. 1982. *The Erosion of Childhood.* Chicago: University of Chicago Press.

Pride, Mary. 1986. *The Child Abuse Industry.* Westchester, IL: Crossway Books.

Sutton, John R. 1988. *Stubborn Children: Controlling Delinquency in the United States, 1640–1981.* Berkeley, CA: University of California Press.

Taylor, Debbie. 1994. *My Children, My Gold.* Berkeley, CA: University of California Press.

Thornton, Yvonne S. 1995. *The Ditchdigger's Daughters.* New York: Birch Lane Press.

Vissing, Yvonne M. 1996. *Out of Sight, Out of Mind.* Lexington, KY: University Press of Kentucky.

16 and 17. Funding Solutions: Parts I and II

Albeda, Randy, Elaine McCrate, Edwin Melendez, June Lapidus. 1988. *Mink Coats Don't Trickle Down.* Boston: South End Press.

———. 1994. *America: Who Really Pays the Taxes?* New York: Touchstone.

Bottomore, Tom, and Robert J. Brym, eds. 1989. *The Capitalist Class: An International Study.* New York: New York University Press.

Clawson, Dan, Alan Neustadtl, Denise Scott. 1992. *Money Talks: Corporate Pacs and Political Influence.* New York: Basic Books.

Cummins, Paul F., co-ed. 1993. "Funding Our Children's Future." California Leadership (April): 11-B Jolly Way, Scotts Valley, CA 95066:

Dale Jr., Edwin L., Jeffrey A. Eisenach, Frank I. Luntz, Timothy J. Muris, William Schneider, Jr. 1995. *The People's Budget.* Washington, D.C.: Regnery Publishing.

Frank, Robert H., and Philip J. Cook. 1995. *The Winner-Take-All Society.* New York: Free Press.

Friedman, Benjamin M. 1989. *Day of Reckoning.* New York: Vintage Books.

Goldsmith, Edward, Robert Allen, Michael Allaby, John Davoll, Sam Lawrence. 1972. "A Blueprint for Survival." *Ecologist Magazine* (January, Vol. II, #1).

Greenberg, Jonathan, and William Kistler, eds. 1992. *Buying America Back.* Tulsa, OK: Council Oak Books.

Greenebaum, Howard. 1990. *Free Elections???* Kelseyville, CA: P.V. Goldsmith.

Makhijani, Arjun. 1992. *From Global Capitalism to Economic Justice.* New York and London: Apex Press.

Martin, Cathie J. 1991. *Shifting the Burden: The Struggle Over Growth and Corporate Taxation.* Chicago: University of Chicago Press.

Odden, Allan R., ed. 1992. *Rethinking School Finance: An Agenda for the 1990s.* San Francisco: Jossey-Bass Publishers.

Reich, Charles A. 1995. *Opposing the System.* New York: Crown Publishers.

Schick, Allen. 1995. *The Federal Budget: Politics, Policy, Process.* Washington, D.C.: Brookings Institute.

Scott, John. 1986. *Capitalist Property and Financial Power: A Comparative Study of Britain, The United States and Japan.* New York: New York University Press.

Thurow, Lester. 1995. "Why Their World Might Crumble." *The New York Times Magazine* (November 19).

18. A Curriculum for the Soul

Bellah, Robert, Richard Madsen, William M. Sullivan, Ann Swidler, Steven M. Tipton. 1996. *Habits of the Heart.* Berkeley: University of California Press.

Bellamy, Edward. 1987. *Looking Backward.* New York: Tickner and Co.

Bowden, Charles. 1995. *Blood Orchid*. New York: Random House.

Calverton, B.F. 1941. *Where Angels Dared to Tread*. New York: Bobbs-Merrill.

Howells, William Dean. 1894. *A Traveler From Altruria*. New York: Harper and Row.

Huffington, Arianna. *The Fourth Instinct: The Call of the Soul*. 1994. New York: Simon and Schuster.

Jung, C.G. 1933. *Modern Man in Search of a Soul*. New York: Harcourt Brace.

————. 1957. *The Undiscovered Self*. Boston: Little Brown.

Momaday, N. Scott. 1966. *House Made of Dawn*. New York: Harper and Row.

Olson, Charles. 1968. *Pleistocene Man: A Curriculum for the Study of the Soul*. Buffalo, New York: Institute of Further Studies.

Schaya, Leo. 1973. *The Universal Meaning of the Kabbalah*. Nancy Pearson, trans. Baltimore, MD: Penguin Books.

Shah, Idries. 1970. *The Way of the Sufi*. New York: E.P. Dutton.

Teilhard de Chardin, Pierre . 1964. *The Future Of Man*. Norman Denny, trans. New York: Harper and Row.

Thoreau, Henry David. 1893–94. *Walden*. Francis H. Allen, ed. Boston, MA: Riverside Editions.

Watts, Alan W. 1961. *Psychotherapy East and West*. New York: Pantheon.

19. Coda

Bellah, Robert, Richard Madsen, William M. Sullivan, Ann Swidler, Steven M. Tipton. 1992. *The Good Society*. New York: Vintage Books.

Herman, Edward S. 1995. *Triumph of the Market*. Bosto: South End Press.

Seabrook, Jeremy. 1993. *Pioneers of Change*. Philadelphia: New Society Publishers.

Sklar, Holly. 1995. *Chaos or Community*. Boston: South End Press.

———— ed. 1980. *Trilateralism: The Trilateral Commission and Elite Planning for World Management*. Boston: South End Press.

Yates, Michael. 1994. *Longer Hours, Fewer Jobs*. New York: Monthly Review Press.

Index

About the Authors

Paul F. Cummins was born in Chicago, moved to Fort Wayne, Indiana, and then to Los Angeles. He attended Stanford (B.A., 1959), Harvard (M.A.T., 1960), and then the University of Southern California (Ph.D., 1967). He has taught English at Harvard School and the Oakwood School in California as well as at U.C.L.A. In 1970, he became Headmaster of St. Augustine's Elementary School in Santa Monica and a founder of the Crossroads School. He is currently President of Crossroads School, grades K through 12, Executive Director of the Crossroads Community Foundation, and Executive Director of the New Visions Foundation.

His publications include a booklet on Richard Wilbur, several articles on education, and numerous poems which have appeared in journals such as *The New Republic, Poetry LA, Whole Notes, Wild Bamboo Press, Bad Haircut Quarterly*, and others. His recent biography on Herbert Zipper, *Dachau Song: The Twentieth-Century Odyssey of Herbert Zipper* (Peter Lang, 1992) has been translated into Chinese and German. He serves on the board of trustees of the Lannan Foundation, American Poetry Review, and the Santa Monica College of Art, Architecture and Design. He and his wife, Mary Ann, live in Santa Monica, California. They have four daughters.

Anna K. Cummins graduated from Crossroads School in Santa Monica in 1991, and Stanford University in 1996 with a B.A. in History. At Stanford, she studied with Dr. Estelle Friedman (Women's Studies), Dr. Jody Maxim (Art History), and Dr. Jack Rakove (American History). Also at Stanford, she was captain of the fencing team in 1994 and performed in chamber music concerts on the violin. She taught at New Roads School, Santa Monica, in 1996, and is currently studying in Spain.